Math Contests
Grades 7 and 8
(and Algebra Course 1)
Volume 7

School Years
2011-2012 through 2015-2016

Written by

Steven R. Conrad • Daniel Flegler • Adam Raichel

Published by MATH LEAGUE PRESS
Printed in the United States of America

Cover art by Bob DeRosa

First Printing, 2016

Math League Press
P.O. Box 17
Tenafly, NJ 07670-0017

ISBN 978-0-940805-22-4

Preface

Math Contests—Grades 7 and 8, Volume 7 is the seventh volume in our series of problem books for grades 7 and 8. The first six volumes contain the contests given in the school years 1979-1980 through 2010-2011. This volume contains the contests given from 2011-2012 through 2015-2016. (You can use the order form on page 154 to order any of our 21 books.)

This book is divided into three sections for ease of use by students and teachers. You'll find the contests in the first section. Each contest consists of 30 or 35 multiple-choice questions that you can do in 30 minutes. On each 3-page contest, the questions on the 1st page are generally straightforward, those on the 2nd page are moderate in difficulty, and those on the 3rd page are more difficult. In the second section of the book, you'll find detailed solutions to all the contest questions. In the third and final section of the book are the letter answers to each contest. In this section, you'll also find rating scales you can use to rate your performance.

Many people prefer to consult the answer section rather than the solution section when first reviewing a contest. We believe that reworking a problem when you know the answer (but *not* the solution) often leads to increased understanding of problem-solving techniques.

Each school year, we sponsor an Annual 7th Grade Mathematics Contest, an Annual 8th Grade Mathematics Contest, and an Annual Algebra Course 1 Mathematics Contest. A student may participate in the contest on grade level or for any higher grade level. For example, students in grade 7 (or below) may participate in the 8th Grade Contest. *Any* student may participate in the Algebra Course 1 Contest. Starting with the 1991-92 school year, students have been permitted to use calculators on any of our contests.

Steven R. Conrad, Daniel Flegler, & Adam Raichel, contest authors

Acknowledgments

For her continued patience and understanding, special thanks to Marina Conrad, whose only mathematical skill, an important one, is the ability to count the ways.

For demonstrating the meaning of selflessness on a daily basis, special thanks to Grace Flegler.

To Jeannine Kolbush, who did an awesome proofreading job, thanks!

Table Of Contents

The Contests

. . . .

2011-2012 through 2015-2016

7th Grade Contests

2011-2012 through 2015-2016

2011-2012 Annual 7th Grade Contest

Tuesday, February 21 or 28, 2012

7

Instructions

- **Time** Do *not* open this booklet until you are told by your teacher to begin. You might be *unable* to finish all 35 questions in the 30 minutes allowed.

- **Scores** Please remember that *this is a contest, and not a test*—there is no "passing" or "failing" score. Few students score as high as 28 points (80% correct). Students with half that, 14 points, *should be commended!*

- **Format, Point Value, & Eligibility** Every answer is an A, B, C, or D. Write answers in the *Answers* column. A correct answer is worth 1 point. Unanswered questions get no credit. You **may** use a calculator.

1. Four million twenty-four thousand divided by 2012 is

    A) 200   B) 2000   C) 2020   D) 20 000

2. The total value of 5 nickels and 5 dimes is the same as the total value of _?_ quarters.

    A) 3   B) 4   C) 5   D) 6

3. What is 0.3456 rounded to the nearest hundredth?

    A) 0.34   B) 0.35   C) 0.345   D) 0.346

4. The sum of all whole-number divisors of 12 is

    A) 0   B) 15   C) 28   D) 56

5. $1^4 + 2^4 + 3^4 =$

    A) 123^4 B) 4^4 C) 6^4 D) $10^2 - 2$

6. The average of $\frac{1}{2}$ and $\frac{1}{4}$ is

    A) $\frac{1}{8}$ B) $\frac{1}{3}$ C) $\frac{3}{8}$ D) $\frac{6}{8}$

7. Billy Beaver chews up 3 pencils per minute while studying. In 2 hours, he chews up _?_ pencils.

    A) 360   B) 180   C) 90   D) 40

8. The average of 21, 34, and 44 is 7 more than the average of 14, 27, and

    A) 37   B) 39   C) 51   D) 79

9. Two sides of a triangle each have length 8. The longest side of the triangle could *not* have length

    A) 8   B) 9   C) 12   D) 16

10. The ratio of boys to girls in class is 4:5. There could be _?_ students.

    A) 45   B) 32   C) 24   D) 20

11. My homework assignment is to read from page 123 through page 321. How many pages of reading have I been assigned?

    A) 198   B) 199   C) 200   D) 201

12. My age 2 years ago plus my age 2 years from now equals 24. How old am I?

    A) 10   B) 12   C) 14   D) 24

13. Tim is hiding between two consecutive pages in his giant book. One of the pages is numbered with the product of 4 different primes. The other page could be

    A) 31   B) 121   C) 129   D) 211

Answers column:
1.
2.
3.
4.
5.
6.
7.
8.
9.
10.
11.
12.
13.

Go on to the next page ⟫➡ **7**

14. Scooter the clown buys flower hats for $27 each and plain hats for $22 each. If he spends a total of $250 on hats, how many hats have flowers?

A) 4   B) 5   C) 6   D) 7

14.

15. 20% of $\frac{2}{3}$ of a quarter of 300 is

A) 10   B) 20   C) 40   D) 50

15.

16. (The reciprocal of $\frac{3}{4}$) ÷ (the reciprocal of $\frac{4}{3}$) =

A) 1   B) $\frac{16}{9}$ C) $\frac{9}{16}$ D) $\frac{3}{4}$

16.

17. The greatest common divisor of 264 and __?__ is 132.

A) 4   B) 66   C) 528   D) 660

17.

18. My dimes and nickels have a total value of $1.00. I have exactly 8 nickels. If I choose a coin at random, the probability that it will be a nickel is

A) $\frac{1}{2}$ B) $\frac{2}{3}$ C) $\frac{4}{3}$ D) $\frac{4}{7}$

18.

19. $((3^4)^4)^4 \div [9^2 \times 9^2 \times 9^2] =$

A) 1   B) 3^6 C) 3^{52} D) 3^{58}

19.

C

20. What time is 10 minutes before 10 hours after 10 A.M.?

A) 7:50 P.M.   B) 9:50 P.M.   C) 11:50 P.M.   D) 4:50 A.M.

20.

21. The wheel on Ed's chair has a radius of 30 cm. If he travels 540π cm, the wheel will rotate __?__ times.

A) 6   B) 9   C) 12   D) 18

21.

22. If a crate of apples contains as many apples as 16 tubs, and 4 tubs of apples contain as many apples as 9 bags, then 3 crates contain as many apples as __?__ bags.

A) 36   B) 72   C) 108   D) 436

22.

23. 20% of 30 is 40% of

A) 15   B) 50   C) 60   D) 90

23.

24. If one angle in a parallelogram has an odd number of degrees, an adjacent angle *cannot* have __?__ number of degrees.

A) an equal   B) an odd   C) a prime   D) a greater

24.

25. Only 10 of my 42 cousins are blond. If 18 of my 24 male cousins are *not* blond, how many of my female cousins are *not* blond?

A) 4   B) 10   C) 12   D) 14

25.

Go on to the next page))) ➡ **7**

26. Ira cries if he hears a number that *cannot* be written as the sum of 2 prime numbers. Ira cries if he hears

    A) 83   B) 99   C) 103   D) 109

26.

27. 0.125% of 25% of 3200 is

    A) 1   B) 10   C) 100   D) 1000

27.

28. The length of a rectangle is three times its width. If the width is an integer, the perimeter *cannot* be

    A) 8   B) 16   C) 32   D) 44

28.

29. $1 \times 2 \times 3 \times \ldots \times 18 \times 19 \times 20$ is divisible by

    A) 23   B) 121   C) 385   D) 580

29.

30. Before yesterday, the average temperature so far this month was 15°. If the average temperature yesterday and today is 40°, and the average for the month is now 20°, then today is the _?_ day of the month.

    A) 8th   B) 10th   C) 12th   D) 16th

30.

31. The ones digit of the sum $1 + 2 + 3 + \ldots + 2011 + 2012$ is

    A) 0   B) 3   C) 8   D) 9

31.

32. Paul wrote his name many times on his pad. When he was finished, the last "u" he wrote could have been the _?_ letter written.

    A) 100th B) 201st C) 302nd D) 403rd

32.

33. After every 3 steps that Pat takes forward, Pat takes 2 steps backward. Each step is 0.5 m. Pat starts at one end of a 50 m hall. Pat will first reach the other end after _?_ steps.

    A) 100   B) 488   C) 490   D) 500

33.

B

34. Gus, Hal, and Jane each try to catch the bus, and their individual probabilities of catching it are $\frac{1}{3}$, $\frac{1}{2}$, and $\frac{2}{5}$, respectively. What is the probability that Gus will catch the bus but Hal and Jane will not?

    A) $\frac{1}{10}$ B) $\frac{1}{15}$ C) $\frac{17}{30}$ D) $\frac{30}{17}$

34.

35. A circle of radius 1 rolls around the outside of a circle of radius 4, always touching the larger circle, and without slipping. How many complete rotations will the smaller circle have made when it returns to its starting position?

    A) 4   B) 5   C) 8   D) 16

35.

B

The end of the contest **7**

2012-2013 Annual 7th Grade Contest

Tuesday, February 19 or 26, 2013

7

Instructions

- **Time** Do *not* open this booklet until you are told by your teacher to begin. You might be *unable* to finish all 35 questions in the 30 minutes allowed.

- **Scores** Please remember that *this is a contest, and not a test*—there is no "passing" or "failing" score. Few students score as high as 28 points (80% correct). Students with half that, 14 points, *should be commended!*

- **Format, Point Value, & Eligibility** Every answer is an A, B, C, or D. Write answers in the *Answers* column. A correct answer is worth 1 point. Unanswered questions get no credit. You **may** use a calculator.

1. Of the following numbers, which is closest to 10.98?   1.

    A) 10.00   B) 10.90   C) 10.95   D) 11.00

2. $\sqrt{4 \times 9 \times 16} =$ 2.

    A) 9   B) 24   C) 29   D) 36

3. Mr. Barry is angry. He has 4 grubs left   3.
    after he tried to divide 256 grubs equally
    among his cubs. There could be ? cubs.

    A) 5   B) 6   C) 8   D) 11

4. The tenths digit of ? is larger than its   4.
    hundredths digit.

    A) 543.21   B) 231.23   C) 654.56   D) 642.46

5. $3^2 + 3^2 + 3^2 =$ 5.

    A) 3^3 B) 3^6 C) 9^3 D) 9^6

6. $3 \div \frac{1}{6} = 9 \div$?   6.

    A) $\frac{1}{18}$ B) $\frac{1}{12}$ C) $\frac{1}{2}$ D) $\frac{9}{2}$

7. The greatest common factor of 2013 and ? is 11.   7.

    A) 231   B) 365   C) 418   D) 542

8. Three times a certain number is 36. One-third of that certain number is 8.

    A) 4   B) 12   C) 36   D) 108

9. If a case of eggs contains 12 dozen eggs, how many eggs are in two   9.
    crates of 12 cases each?   ▷

    A) 48   B) 144   C) 288   D) 3456

10. One hundred million divided by ten thousand equals   10.
    A) 10   B) 100   C) 1000   D) 10 000

11. Ashley the chimney sweep puts his hat down on a   11.
    square the same size as the opening of a chimney.
    The circular brim touches each side of the square at a
    single point. The perimeter of the square is 4 m. What
    is the radius of the circular brim of Ashley's hat?

    A) 0.5 m B) 1 m   C) 2 m   D) 4 m

12. $\frac{1}{3} \times \frac{2}{4} \times \frac{3}{5} \times \frac{4}{6} \times \frac{5}{7} \times \frac{6}{8} \times \frac{7}{9} \times \frac{8}{10} = \frac{1}{10} \times$?   12.

    A) $\frac{3}{19}$ B) $\frac{2}{9}$ C) $\frac{1}{9}$ D) $\frac{2}{90}$

13. $20 + 30 + 40 -$ (the average of 20, 30, and 40) =   13.

    A) 0   B) 45   C) 60   D) 90

Go on to the next page))⟩ **7**

14. Del loves sandwiches so much that 130 of his last 250 meals were sandwiches. What percent of those last 250 meals were *not* sandwiches?

   A) 40% B) 44% C) 48% D) 52%

14.

15. The sum of the two least odd divisors of 120 is

   A) 4 B) 5 C) 8 D) 15

15.

16. I collect 20 seashells every 30 minutes, but I drop 3 shells every 2 hours. If I collect shells for 8 hours, I will end up with __?__ shells.

   A) 68 B) 136 C) 296 D) 308

16.

17. The number of nickels in $3.00 plus the number of dimes in $6.00 is half the number of quarters in

   A) $12.00 B) $15.00 C) $30.00 D) $60.00

17.

D

18. 0.05% of 10000 equals

   A) 5 B) 50 C) 500 D) 5000

18.

19. The sum of 13 consecutive integers is 13. The greatest of the integers is

   A) 6 B) 7 C) 9 D) 13

19.

20. Apples cost 65¢ each and oranges cost 85¢ each. If I spend $8.80 on apples and oranges, how many pieces of fruit did I buy all together?

   A) 11 B) 12 C) 13 D) 14

20.

21. Dragon Doug reads a prime number of books each month. If each prime is different, which of the following *cannot* be the total number of books he reads in 3 months?

   A) 10 B) 12 C) 13 D) 15

21.

22. The number halfway between 45674567 and 67896789 is

   A) 55443322 B) 55556666
   C) 56565656 D) 56785678

22.

23. $\sqrt{49} - \sqrt{16} =$

   A) $\sqrt{33}$ B) $\sqrt{25}$ C) $\sqrt{9}$ D) $\sqrt{3}$

23.

24. The greatest power of 3 that divides 2016^{2013} is

   A) 3^{2013} B) 3^{2015} C) 3^{4026} D) 3^{6039}

24.

25. A new spa opens for the first time on Wednesday, March 2. If it is open only on Monday through Friday each week, its 21st day open will be

   A) March 22 B) March 23 C) March 30 D) March 31

25.

Go on to the next page))) **7**

26. Wilma's potion needs 3 ingredients. Her choices are newt, fly, beetle, snake, and snail. How many different combinations of 3 of these 5 choices are there?

A) 6   B) 8   C) 10   D) 60

26.

27. The sum of six consecutive integers *could* be

A) 81   B) 88   C) 92   D) 98

27.

28. 288 minutes = _?_ % of 1 day

A) 10   B) 15   C) 20   D) 40

28.

29. Two cousins visited Jane today. One cousin visits every 42 days. The other visits every 429 days. They will next visit on the same day in _?_ days.

A) 4296   B) 6006   C) 9009   D) 18018

29.

30. $3^{2013} - 3^{2012} =$

A) 3^1 B) 3^{2011} C) 2×3^{2012} D) 6^{1006}

30.

31. The measure of the smaller angle formed by the hour and minute hands of a circular clock at 2:46 is

A) 84°   B) 137°   C) 167°   D) 174°

31.

32. The median of $\frac{1}{6}, \frac{2}{5}, \frac{3}{4}, \frac{4}{3}, \frac{5}{2}$, and $\frac{6}{1}$ is

A) 1   B) $\frac{669}{360}$ C) $\frac{7}{12}$ D) $\frac{25}{24}$

32.

33. Brad mixes seeds to attract birds. His Blue mix is 55% sunflower and 45% bluegrass. His Rye mix is 30% sunflower and 70% ryegrass. His Master mix combines some of each of the Blue and Rye mixes. If Master mix is 45% sunflower, how much of each kg of Master mix is Blue mix?

A) 350 g   B) 400 g   C) 600 g   D) 650 g

33.

C

34. If I multiply all whole numbers from 1 through 100, the largest power of 4 that is a factor of the product is

A) 4^{25} B) 4^{32} C) 4^{48} D) 4^{50}

34.

C

35. Of my books, 85% are new and the rest are used. Some are biographies, 70% of which are new. What is the ratio of the fraction of new books that are biographies to the fraction of used books that are biographies?

A) 7:17   B) 14:17   C) 17:14   D) 17:7

35.

A

The end of the contest ✍ **7**

Visit our Web site at http://www.mathleague.com
Solutions on Page 77 • Answers on Page 139

12

2013-2014 Annual 7th Grade Contest

Tuesday, February 18 or 25, 2014

7

Instructions

- **Time** Do *not* open this booklet until you are told by your teacher to begin. You might be *unable* to finish all 35 questions in the 30 minutes allowed.

- **Scores** Please remember that *this is a contest, and not a test*—there is no "passing" or "failing" score. Few students score as high as 28 points (80% correct). Students with half that, 14 points, *should be commended!*

- **Format, Point Value, & Eligibility** Every answer is an A, B, C, or D. Write answers in the *Answers* column. A correct answer is worth 1 point. Unanswered questions get no credit. You **may** use a calculator.

	Answers
1. $2014 \times 2 = 2014 \times 4 \underline{\ ?\ } 2014 \times 2$ A) – B) + C) × D) ÷	1.
2. Mr. Spud is the world's slowest potato inspector. He inspects 20 potatoes per hour, 8 hours per day. In 5 days he inspects a total of _?_ potatoes. A) 33 B) 160 C) 165 D) 800	2.
3. $2 \times 3 \times 4 \times 5 \div \underline{\ ?\ } = 12$ A) 6 B) 8 C) 10 D) 12	3.
4. I am 20th in line and my friend is 10th in line. How many people are between us? A) 8 B) 9 C) 10 D) 11	4.
5. There are 24 socks in a drawer, and exactly half are black socks. How many *pairs* of black socks are in the drawer? A) 4 B) 6 C) 12 D) 24	5.
6. Which of the following figures has an odd number of sides? A) rhombus B) trapezoid C) pentagon D) hexagon	6.
7. $5 + 25 + 125 = 5 \times \underline{\ ?\ }$ A) 6 B) 15 C) 25 D) 31	7.
8. For how many integers from 55 to 66 is the ones digit greater than the tens digit? A) 4 B) 5 C) 10 D) 11	8.
9. Of the following, which leaves a remainder of 2 when divided by 3? A) 371 B) 456 C) 523 D) 676	9.
10. Lex buys 6 same-priced books and pays with a $50 bill. The change Lex receives is twice the price of a book. Each book costs A) $6.25 B) $7.14 C) $8.33 D) $12.50	10.
11. Sam skateboarded until the sun set at 6:16 PM. Sam skateboarded for 66 minutes. Sam's skateboarding started at what time? A) 5:00 P.M. B) 5:10 P.M. C) 5:22 P.M. D) 5:30 P.M.	11.
12. In what month is the 222nd day of the year? A) May B) June C) July D) August	12. D
13. Each side of a square is equal in length to a side of an equilateral triangle of perimeter 18. What is the perimeter of the square? A) 18 B) 24 C) 36 D) 90	13.

Go on to the next page ⫸ **7**

14

14. The number of heart balloons that Cora has is divisible by three different primes. What is the least number of heart balloons that Cora can have?

A) 6   B) 10   C) 15   D) 30

14.

15. The ones digit of the greatest multiple of 13 that is less than 10 000 is

A) 3   B) 6   C) 7   D) 9

15.

16. 10 quarters + 30 dimes = _?_ nickels

A) 50   B) 60   C) 100   D) 110

16.

17. If 2 quonks = 6 quinks and 3 quinks = 8 quanks, then _?_ quonks = 64 quanks.

A) 8   B) 16   C) 24   D) 32

17.

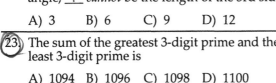

18. The average of 2014 sixes is equal to the average of 4028 _?_ .

A) threes   B) sixes   C) nines   D) twelves

18.

19. How many whole-number factors of 120 are divisible by 3?

A) 7   B) 8   C) 9   D) 10

19.

$\mathcal{B}$

20. What is 0.625% of 8% of 500?

A) 0.25   B) 2.5   C) 25   D) 250

20.

21. Dr. Craven is very nervous about his speech because he sees that for every 2 people in the audience who are smiling, there are 7 who are not. How many people might be in the audience?

A) 77   B) 85   C) 99   D) 105

21.

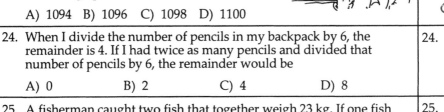

22. If 5 and 9 are the lengths of two sides of a triangle, _?_ *cannot* be the length of the 3rd side.

A) 3   B) 6   C) 9   D) 12

22.

23. The sum of the greatest 3-digit prime and the least 3-digit prime is

A) 1094   B) 1096   C) 1098   D) 1100

23.

C

24. When I divide the number of pencils in my backpack by 6, the remainder is 4. If I had twice as many pencils and divided that number of pencils by 6, the remainder would be

A) 0   B) 2   C) 4   D) 8

24.

25. A fisherman caught two fish that together weigh 23 kg. If one fish weighs 5 kg less than the other, the heavier fish weighs

A) 9 kg   B) 12 kg   C) 14 kg   D) 19 kg

25.

Go on to the next page)))➡ **7**

26. If $\frac{1}{5}$ of the 200 stripes on Frank's giant shell are blue, $\frac{2}{5}$ of the remaining stripes are brown, and the rest are white, there are __?__ more white stripes than blue.

    A) 0   B) 40   C) 42   D) 56

26.

D

27. If 125% of a number is 160, 75% of the number is

    A) 82   B) 88   C) 90   D) 96

27.

28. The sum of the squares of 2 integers each greater than 0 is $17^2 = 289$. The sum of these 2 integers is

    A) 23   B) 25   C) 27   D) 29

28.

29. If $\frac{1}{13}$ is written as a decimal, the 100th digit after the decimal point is

    A) 9   B) 6   C) 3   D) 2

29.

30. Bei's and Fay's ages average 12, and Ray's and Clyde's ages average 16. If Bei's, Fay's, and Ray's ages average 11, how old is Clyde?

    A) 28   B) 23   C) 20   D) 17

30.

31. Kim has red, blue, grey, orange, yellow, and white paints. If she picks 3 of them for a painting but never uses red and blue in the same painting, there are __?__ 3-color combinations she could use.

    A) 16   B) 32   C) 64   D) 120

31.

32. $\dfrac{5^{95} - 5^{94}}{2^2} =$

    A) 1.25   B) $5^{91} - 5^{90}$ C) $5^{93} - 5^{92}$ D) 5^{94}

32.

33. Professor Stache awarded 500 certificates, some for math and some for science. Girls won 2/3 of the math certificates and 1/2 of the science certificates. If the number of girls who won for math was 50 more than 3/2 the number of girls who won for science, how many girls won for math?

    A) 200   B) 275   C) 300   D) 350

33.

34. Each vertex of square S is on a different side of a square of side-length 20. The least possible area of S is

    A) 100   B) 160   C) 200   D) 250

34.

C

35. The sequence 72, 75, 76, 81, 84, 85, . . . , in which each new number is 9 greater than the number that is 3 numbers before it, includes

    A) 694   B) 733   C) 812   D) 950

35.

The end of the contest ✍ **7**

2014-2015 Annual 7th Grade Contest

Tuesday, February 17 or February 24, 2015

7

Instructions

- **Time** Do *not* open this booklet until you are told by your teacher to begin. You might be *unable* to finish all 35 questions in the 30 minutes allowed.

- **Scores** Please remember that *this is a contest, and not a test*—there is no "passing" or "failing" score. Few students score as high as 28 points (80% correct). Students with half that, 14 points, *should be commended!*

- **Format, Point Value, & Eligibility** Every answer is an A, B, C, or D. Write answers in the *Answers* column. A correct answer is worth 1 point. Unanswered questions get no credit. You **may** use a calculator.

$\times 4 - 2 \times 0 + 1 \times 5 =$ | 1.

, ບ B) 5 C) 9 D) 15

---

2. There are 84 beavers in a colony. Yesterday they all went out in teams of 6 to collect logs. Today they are all going out in teams of 4. There will be __?__ more teams today than there were yesterday.

A) 2 B) 7 C) 14 D) 21

| 2.

---

3. $12\,345 + 54\,321 = 11\,111 \times$ __?__

A) 66 666 B) 666 C) 66 D) 6

| 3.

---

4. My brother is exactly twice my age, and he is 192 months old. I am __?__ years old.

A) 8 B) 16 C) 32 D) 96

| 4.

---

5. Apples cost $1.25 each, or 3 for $3. If I want to buy 11 apples, I need at *least* how much money?

A) $11.00 B) $11.50 C) $12.00 D) $13.75

| 5.

---

6. Multiplying a number by $\frac{2}{3}$ is the same as dividing it by

A) 0.667 B) 0.75 C) 1.5 D) 1.667

| 6.

---

7. How many prime factors of 120 are multiples of 4?

A) 0 B) 6 C) 7 D) 8

| 7.

---

8. I have test scores of 80, 84, and 94, and I want my average test score to be 86 after my next test. What score must I get on the next test?

A) 0 B) 86 C) 87 D) 88

| 8.

---

9. The lengths of the sides of a triangle are consecutive even integers. Which of the following *cannot* be the length of the longest side?

A) 6 B) 10 C) 12 D) 16

| 9.

---

10. Nigel has the volume set at 8, but it goes to 10. He could increase the volume by at most __?__.

A) 2% B) 10% C) 20% D) 25%

| 10.

---

11. $75^2 \times 25 = 25^2 \times$ __?__

A) 3^2 B) 5^2 C) 75 D) 15^2

| 11.

---

12. The sum of two different primes *cannot* be

A) odd B) even C) 123 D) a perfect square

| 12.

---

13. The product of a circle's circumference and radius divided by its area is

A) 2 B) π C) 2π D) $2\pi^2$

| 13.

---

14. Mr. Wells is becoming invisible. Today he is 100% visible, but each morning from tomorrow on he will wake to find himself 80% as visible as he had been the day before. He will first be less than 50% visible in __?__ days.

A) 3   B) 4   C) 5   D) 6

14.

15. $1\frac{1}{3} \times 1\frac{1}{4} \times 1\frac{1}{5} =$

A) 2   B) 3   C) $1\frac{1}{6}$ D) $1\frac{1}{60}$

15.

16. The largest prime factor of $1\,000\,000\,000$ is

A) 1   B) 2   C) 5   D) 10

16.

17. $999\,999 \times 999\,998 = 999\,999^2 -$ __?__

A) 1   B) 999\,997   C) 999\,998   D) 999\,999

17.

18. Eight years from now, I will be twice my age two years ago. How old will I be two years from now?

A) 14   B) 16   C) 18   D) 20

18.

19. The combined value of my quarters and nickels is ten times the combined value of my pennies and nickels. If I have the same number of pennies as nickels, my ratio of quarters to pennies is

A) 1:1   B) 2:1   C) 10:3   D) 11:5

19.

20. How many fractions equal to 0.75 have numerators and denominators that are positive integers less than 100?

A) 3   B) 24   C) 25   D) 33

20.

21. The Skippers have been rowing a raft for 5 hours. In each hour after the first, they row 2 km less than they rowed the hour before. If their average rowing rate is 6 km/hr, they traveled __?__ km during the first 2 hours.

A) 6   B) 12   C) 16   D) 18

21.

22. 500 is __?__% greater than 200.

A) 50   B) 150   C) 250   D) 300

22.

23. Between 100 and 1000, __?__ numbers are squares of odd integers.

A) 11   B) 16   C) 21   D) 31

23.

24. A square of perimeter 360 consists of exactly __?__ squares of area 9.

A) 40   B) 400   C) 900   D) 1600

24.

25. The largest odd factor of $6^6 \times 10^{10}$ is

A) $6^5 \times 10^9$ B) $6^3 \times 10^5$ C) $3^6 \times 5^{10}$ D) $3^3 \times 5^5$

25.

26. Greg finished senior year without learning how to type! His friend Ori charged him $4 per page the first time a page was typed, and $2 each time a page was redone. Ori typed 150 pages, then redid 30 pages, and finally redid 15 pages a 2nd time. The total cost to Greg was

   A) $660   B) $690   C) $720   D) $760

26.

27. What fraction of the factors of 10^2 are factors of 10?

   A) $\dfrac{1}{10}$ B) $\dfrac{4}{9}$ C) $\dfrac{5}{9}$ D) $\dfrac{9}{10}$

27.

28. Which of the following sums is equal to a prime number?

   A) $29^2 + 66^2$ B) $42^2 + 45^2$ C) $22^2 + 64^2$ D) $32^2 + 54^2$

28.

29. If the square shown is rotated 1890° counterclockwise, side _?_ will be at the top.

   A) A   B) B   C) C   D) D

29.

30. The least common multiple of 2^2, 4^2, 6^2, 8^2, and 10^2 is

   A) 3840   B) 14 400   C) 57 600   D) 230 400

30.

31. A snail crawls 2400 mm per hour. It takes _?_ seconds to crawl 1 mm.

   A) $\dfrac{1}{3}$ B) $\dfrac{2}{3}$ C) 1.5   D) 3

31.

32. A circle can intersect a quadrilateral at _?_ points.

   A) 0, 2 or 8 only   B) 0, 2, 4, 6 or 8 only
   C) 1, 2, 3, 4, 6, or 8 only   D) 0, 1, 2, 3, 4, 5, 6, 7, or 8

32.

33. Carla loves shells! She collects them, labelling each with a 1-, 2-, or 3-letter code. If the same letters are used in a different order, it is a different code. She has used every such code, so she has _?_ shells.

   A) 156   B) 17576   C) 18278   D) 20888

33.

34. If the sum of 50 consecutive integers is 1525, what is the sum of the next 50 consecutive integers?

   A) 1575   B) 2775   C) 4025   D) 76250

34.

35. Of 4 pairs of twins, 3 students are chosen to do a report together. There are _?_ possible groups of 3 that don't include both twins from a pair.

   A) 16   B) 24   C) 28   D) 32

35.

The end of the contest ✍ **7**

2015-2016 Annual 7th Grade Contest

Tuesday, February 16 or February 23, 2016

7

Instructions

- **Time** Do *not* open this booklet until you are told by your teacher to begin. You might be *unable* to finish all 35 questions in the 30 minutes allowed.

- **Scores** Please remember that *this is a contest, and not a test*—there is no "passing" or "failing" score. Few students score as high as 28 points (80% correct). Students with half that, 14 points, *should be commended!*

- **Format, Point Value, & Eligibility** Every answer is an A, B, C, or D. Write answers in the *Answers* column. A correct answer is worth 1 point. Unanswered questions get no credit. You **may** use a calculator.

1. $(2 + 0 + 1 + 6) \times (6 + 1 + 0 + 2) =$

     A) 3^2 B) 3^3 C) 3^4 D) 3^6

1.

2. Of the 77 7th graders in my school, $\frac{3}{7}$ are boys. How many are girls?

     A) 30   B) 33   C) 40   D) 44

2.

3. $2016000000 = 2.016 \times \underline{\ ?\ }$

     A) 10^6 B) 10^7 C) 10^8 D) 10^9

3.

4. The time I spent on math was half the time I spent on English. If English took 9000 seconds, math took $\underline{\ ?\ }$ minutes.

     A) 15   B) 45   C) 75   D) 150

4.

5. Adding –5 to a number is the same as subtracting $\underline{\ ?\ }$ from the number.

     A) 5   B) -5   C) 1/5   D) -1/5

5.

6. The reciprocal of $\underline{\ ?\ }$ is not an integer.

     A) 0.2   B) 0.4   C) 0.5   D) 1

6.

7. $80 \times 36 + 80 \times 14 = 80 \times \underline{\ ?\ }$

     A) 50   B) 60   C) 130   D) 504

7.

8. How many of the first 2016 positive integers are squares of integers?

     A) 43   B) 44   C) 45   D) 46

8.

9. What is the greatest prime number less than 100 that can itself be expressed as the sum of two prime numbers?

     A) 91   B) 89   C) 79   D) 73

9.

D

10. For which of the following pairs is the least common multiple greatest?

     A) 7 and 8   B) 4 and 11   C) 12 and 16   D) 6 and 36

10.

A

11. If I travel at 6 m/sec, I will get home in 4 minutes. If I travel at 8 m/sec, the trip will take how many *fewer* minutes?

     A) 1   B) 3   C) 4   D) 60

11.

12. The product of 49 and a perfect square must be

     A) prime   B) odd
     C) even   D) a perfect square

12.

13. $3 \times 9 \times 27 =$

     A) 3^3 B) 3^4 C) 3^5 D) 3^6

13.

Go on to the next page ⟫➡ **7**

14. When Jen shouts "30," her toy, Squaroo, says, "30, 5, 2, 1." The first number is the one Jen shouts, and each number after the first is the greatest integer that does not exceed the square root of the prior number. Squaroo stops once it says "1." If Jen shouts "10 000," how many numbers does Squaroo say?

   A) 4   B) 5   C) 6   D) 7

   14. *5*

15. How many different positive integers are factors of both 2015 and 2016?

   A) 1   B) 2   C) 3   D) 4

   15.

16. Which of the following is a prime?

   A) 2015   B) 2016   C) 2017   D) 2018

   16.

17. If the last 3 digits of an integer are 864, the integer must be divisible by

   A) 3   B) 6   C) 8   D) 9

   17.

18. In Joe's class, the ratio of boys to girls is 5:7. If there are 10 more girls than boys in the class, Joe's class has __?__ boys.

   A) 25   B) 30   C) 35   D) 40

   18.

19. If the side-length of square A is 4 and the area of square B is 9 times that of square A, what is the perimeter of square B?

   A) 12   B) 36   C) 48   D) 144

   19.

20. The 5th power of a prime has __?__ different positive integer factors.

   A) 5   B) 6   C) 32   D) 120

   20. *B.*

21. $111 \times 89 = 100^2 - \underline{\ ?\ }$

   A) 10   B) 11   C) 100   D) 121

   21.

22. How many integers between 1 and 500 have a remainder of 2 when divided by 4?

   A) 122   B) 123   C) 124   D) 125

   22.

23. If the sum of two prime numbers is 24, their product *cannot* be

   A) 63   B) 95   C) 119   D) 143

   23.

24. Multiplying the length of each side of a square by 1.5 increases its area by

   A) 25%   B) 50%   C) 125%   D) 225%

   24. *D*

25. How many 3-digit positive integers have 5 as the product of their digits?

   A) 4   B) 3   C) 2   D) 1

   25.

Go on to the next page ⟫➡ **7**

23

26. There are 124 gumballs in a machine. The product of the 1st and 3rd digits of the integer 124 is equal to the square of its 2nd digit. What is the least number of additional gumballs that would have to be added for the new number of gumballs in the machine to have this same property?

    A) 209   B) 124   C) 98   D) 15

26.

27. What is the sum of 1 and all positive factors of 2^8?

    A) 2^8 B) 2^9 C) 2^{10} D) 2^{11}

27.

28. At Minimalist College, every student is required to study either math or English. If 60 students study math, 70 students study English, and 30 students study both, how many students attend Minimalist?

    A) 100   B) 130   C) 160   D) 190

28.

29. The lengths of two sides of a triangle are 20 and 35. How many different positive integers can be the length of the third side?

    A) 37   B) 38   C) 39   D) 40

29.

30. If all the digits of a prime are 1s, the prime may have __?__ digits

    A) 19   B) 21   C) 22   D) 25

30.
A

31. What is the ones digit of $2016^{2016} + 2017^{2017}$?

    A) 3   B) 5   C) 7   D) 9

31.

32. What is the fewest number of people that must attend a party to be sure that four of them have birthdays in the same calendar month?

    A) 15   B) 16   C) 36   D) 37

32.
D

33. The greatest prime factor of $9^{1010} - 3^{2016}$ is

    A) 3   B) 5   C) 7   D) 13

33.
B

34. The sum of all integers between 1000 and 10 000 with all odd digits is

    A) 138 875   B) 694 375   C) 3 471 875   D) 17 359 375

34.
C

35. If 7 different circles are drawn to maximize the number of points at which 2 or more circles intersect, there are __?__ points of intersection.

    A) 20   B) 30   C) 35   D) 42

35.

The end of the contest ☜ **7**

8th Grade Contests

2011-2012 through 2015-2016

2011-2012 Annual 8th Grade Contest

Tuesday, February 21 or 28, 2012

8

Instructions

- **Time** Do *not* open this booklet until you are told by your teacher to begin. You might be *unable* to finish all 35 questions in the 30 minutes allowed.

- **Scores** Please remember that *this is a contest, and not a test*—there is no "passing" or "failing" score. Few students score as high as 28 points (80% correct). Students with half that, 14 points, *should be commended!*

- **Format, Point Value, & Eligibility** Every answer is an A, B, C, or D. Write answers in the *Answers* column. A correct answer is worth 1 point. Unanswered questions get no credit. You **may** use a calculator.

1. Explorer Rick sees 2012 animals. Half are 2-legged and half are 4-legged. How many legs does Rick see?

   A) 4024 B) 6036 C) 8048 D) 12072

   1.

2. $1000 \div 100 + 10 \times 0 =$

   A) 0   B) 10   C) 100   D) 1000

   2.

3. Which of the following numbers is greatest?

   A) 0.123 B) 0.321 C) 0.0123 D) 0.0321

   3.

4. When I count from 1 to 20, what percent of the numbers that I count are prime?

   A) 8%   B) 9%   C) 40%   D) 45%

   4.

5. Five brothers were born on the same month and day in five consecutive years. If today is their birthday, and the oldest brother is twice as old as the youngest, how old is the middle brother?

   A) 3   B) 4   C) 5   D) 6

   5.

6. If I multiply the ten years 2011, 2012, 2013, . . . , 2020, what is the ones digit of the product?

   A) 0   B) 1   C) 5   D) 9

   6.

7. Two sides of a triangle have length 7. If the third side is not longer than 7, then the triangle could *not* be

   A) isosceles   B) equilateral   C) acute   D) right

   7.

8. 20% of 50 =

   A) 2% of 0.5   B) 5% of 0.2   C) 200% of 5   D) 500% of 20

   8.

9. Sheriff Sam's slingshot slings berries weighing 0.7 g each. If his slingshot slings 70 kg of berries, how many berries does Sheriff Sam's slingshot sling?

   A) 1000 B) 10000 C) 100000 D) 1000000

   9.

10. I worked for a "month of Sundays," which is 30 consecutive Sundays and all the days between them. In all, I worked for _?_ days.

    A) 210 B) 204 C) 198   D) 192

    10.

11. If $\frac{2}{3}$ of a certain number is 200, then $\frac{3}{2}$ of that certain number is

    A) 200 B) 400 C) 450   D) 600

    11.

12. The average of 100, -100, 200, -200, and 300 is

    A) 60   B) 150   C) 200   D) 300

    12.

Go on to the next page)))) **8**

13. From the spot I started walking east, I dropped a rock every 8 m, a coin | 13.
    every 12 m, and a frog every 18 m. How far had I walked the first time
    I dropped one of each at the same distance from my starting point?

    A) 38 m   B) 72 m   C) 128 m   D) 1728 m

14. $\frac{2}{3} + \frac{4}{5} = \frac{66}{?}$ | 14.

    A) 15   B) 30   C) 45   D) 88

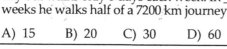

15. A singer walks 5 km/hr. He walks 8 hours per | 15.
    day but walks only 6 days each week. In _?_
    weeks he walks half of a 7200 km journey.

    A) 15   B) 20   C) 30   D) 60

16. The total number of faces and edges of a cube is | 16.

    A) 12   B) 14   C) 16   D) 18

17. My lemonade recipe requires $\frac{3}{2}$ ℓ of water and makes 2 dozen servings. | 17.
    Based on this recipe, how much water do I need to make 30 servings?

    A) $\frac{7}{8}$ ℓ   B) $\frac{15}{8}$ ℓ   C) $\frac{7}{4}$ ℓ   D) $\frac{15}{4}$ ℓ

18. I have 30 nickels and 10 quarters. The average value of these coins is | 18.

    A) 10¢   B) 15¢   C) 20¢   D) 30¢

19. Which of the following numbers is closest in value to its own | 19.
    reciprocal?

    A) 1.001   B) 1.01   C) 1.111   D) 1.2

20. Of 56 dogs, 34 have spots, 23 have blue eyes, and 11 have neither. | 20.
    How many have both blue eyes and spots?

    A) 6   B) 12   C) 24   D) 31

21. Cy's umbrella lifted him off the ground after he lost | 21.
    20% of his weight. He dropped from _?_ kg to 40 kg.

    A) 42   B) 44   C) 48   D) 50

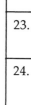

22. The product of 3 integers is 60. Their sum *cannot* be | 22.

    A) 12   B) 15   C) 18   D) 22

23. If n is an integer, then _?_ must be even. | 23.

    A) $n+1$ B) $n+2$ C) $2 \times n+1$ D) $2 \times n+2$

24. $(200^3 \times 200^3)^6 \div 200^9 =$ | 24.

    A) 200^4 B) 200^6 C) 200^{27} D) 200^{45}

25. Which positive integer's only positive factors are 1, 5, 13, 25, 65, and itself? | 25.

    A) 325   B) 845   C) 1625   D) 105 625

Go on to the next page)))➡ **8**

26. It cost Darius Dog 60 bones per painting to buy one-eighth of all the paintings in his collection. It cost him 90 bones per painting for the other 56 paintings in his collection. His collection cost him __?__ bones.

   A) 5340   B) 5400   C) 5460   D) 5520

26.

27. A string of length 100π is cut into 2 pieces, and each piece is formed into a circle. If one of the circles has area 64π, the other circle has area

   A) 36π B) 56π C) 136π D) 1764π

27.

28. Points P, Q, R, and S lie in a straight line (though not necessarily in that order). The distance from P to Q is 4, from Q to R is 5, and from R to S is 6. Which of the following *cannot* be the distance from P to S?

   A) 3   B) 5   C) 7   D) 9

28.

29. $21^{21} + 21^{22} =$

   A) 21^{43} B) $21^{21} \times 22$ C) $2 \times 21^{21} + 21$ D) $2 \times 21^{22} - 21$

29.

30. If the sum of the digits of a certain two-digit integer is multiplied by 4, the product is the original integer. How many such integers exist?

   A) 1   B) 2   C) 4   D) 8

30.

31. In the diagram (not drawn to scale), if $BC = 8$ and $m\angle A = m\angle DBA = 2 \times m\angle C$, then $AD =$

   A) 4   B) 8   C) 12   D) 16

31.

32. If I want to be 850 m from where I am now on a flat surface, I *cannot* go

   A) 238 m north, then 816 m east   B) 510 m north, then 680 m east
   C) 360 m north, then 780 m east   D) 400 m north, then 750 m east

32.

33. How many positive three-digit integers include no digits other than the digits 6, 7, or 8?

   A) 6   B) 9   C) 18   D) 27

33.

34. The ratio of Will's integral height to a giant dart's integral height is 2:5. If Will were 20 cm shorter and the dart were 20 cm taller, the ratio would be 1:3. Will's height now is how much less than the dart's?

   A) 240 cm B) 260 cm   C) 280 cm D) 320 cm

34.

35. I am thinking of three different 2-digit whole numbers. The ones digits of two of the numbers are equal, and the tens digits of two of the numbers are equal. How many different sets of three such numbers are possible?

   A) 6480   B) 7200   C) 7290   D) 8100

35.

Visit our Web site at http://www.mathleague.com
Solutions on Page 95 • Answers on Page 143

2012-2013 Annual 8th Grade Contest

Tuesday, February 19 or 26, 2013

8

Instructions

- **Time** Do *not* open this booklet until you are told by your teacher to begin. You might be *unable* to finish all 35 questions in the 30 minutes allowed.

- **Scores** Please remember that *this is a contest, and not a test*—there is no "passing" or "failing" score. Few students score as high as 28 points (80% correct). Students with half that, 14 points, *should be commended!*

- **Format, Point Value, & Eligibility** Every answer is an A, B, C, or D. Write answers in the *Answers* column. A correct answer is worth 1 point. Unanswered questions get no credit. You **may** use a calculator.

1. $(1 + 4 + 1 + 4) \times \underline{} = 14\,140$

   A) 10   B) 1010   C) 1414   D) 10\,000

   1.

2. The number of fish in a giant sandwich is divisible by 2, 3, 4, and 5.
   There could be _?_ fish.

   A) 2345   B) 4567
   C) 5550   D) 6660

   2.

3. The average of 25 and _?_ is 2013.

   A) 994   B) 1019   C) 1988   D) 4001

   3.

4. Bob rides his bicycle at 40 km per hour. How far will Bob ride in 3
   minutes?

   A) 1 km   B) 2 km   C) 3 km   D) 4 km

   4.

5. I am waiting in line with 10 people in front of me, including my
   brother. My brother has 10 people behind him in line, including me.
   If my brother is right in front of me, how many people are in line?

   A) 11   B) 19   C) 20   D) 21

   5.

6. Each of my 60 books has either a hard cover or a soft cover. If I have
   4 times as many hard covers as soft covers, I have _?_ hard covers.

   A) 48   B) 35   C) 15   D) 12

   6.

7. The largest odd factor of 111 is

   A) 3   B) 37   C) 109   D) 111

   7.

8. My coin jar has 100 pennies, 200 nickels, 300 dimes, and 400 quarters
   in it. The coins have a total value of

   A) $91   B) $121   C) $141   D) $161

   8.

9. The hundreds digit of the product $123\,456\,789 \times 234\,567\,890$ is

   A) 0   B) 1   C) 2   D) 3

   9.

10. Ben finds a pair of eyes under 40% of
    the rocks he checks. If he looks under
    400 rocks, he will find _?_ eyes.

    A) 100   B) 160   C) 200   D) 320

    10.

11. $12 \times \dfrac{1}{2} \times \dfrac{1}{3} \times \dfrac{1}{4} \times \dfrac{1}{6} =$

    A) $\dfrac{1}{144}$ B) $\dfrac{1}{12}$ C) 1   D) 12

    11.

12. If the measures of the angles of triangle T are in a 1:2:3 ratio, what
    kind of triangle is T?

    A) acute   B) obtuse   C) right   D) isosceles

    12.

Go on to the next page))))⟩ **8**

13. Of the following, which is greatest?

A) $9 + 8 \times 6 - 4 \div 2$ B) $(9 + 8) \times 6 - 4 \div 2$

C) $9 + 8 \times (6 - 4) \div 2$ D) $(9 + 8) \times (6 - 4) \div 2$

13.

14. Coal miner Axel found diamonds! If the number of diamonds Axel found was the least common multiple of 18, 28, and 38, he found __?__ diamonds.

A) 2   B) 84   C) 4788   D) 19 152

14.

15. 7 hundredths + 7 thousandths = 7 tenths − __?__

A) 0.623   B) 0.777   C) 0.784   D) 0.854

15.

16. $2^2 \times 2^2 \times 2^2 + 2^2 \times 2^2 + 2^2 = 2^2 \times$ __?__

A) 16   B) 21   C) 32   D) 33

16.

17. If I multiply the number of math contests I have taken in my life by 6 and then add 5, the resulting number *cannot* be divisible by

A) 5   B) 7   C) 9   D) 11

17.

18. An evil witch casts a spell to put a princess to sleep for 10 000 hours. If the princess falls asleep at 6:00 P.M., she will wake at

A) 10:00 A.M.   B) 4:00 P.M.   C) 8:00 P.M.   D) 11:00 P.M.

18.

19. Of the rocks in a box, 1/3 are igneous, 60 are metamorphic, and the remaining 40% are sedimentary. How many rocks are in the box?

A) 160   B) 180   C) 200   D) 225

19.

20. The sum of 4 consecutive even integers is 148. The sum of the digits of the smallest of the 4 integers is

A) 6   B) 7   C) 9   D) 12

20.

21. Max has 9 pairs of glasses for every 2 surfboards he has. If he has 108 pairs of glasses, he has __?__ surfboards.

A) 12   B) 24   C) 48   D) 486

21.

22. 180 + 150% of 180 =

A) 270   B) 330   C) 450   D) 630

22.

23. The perimeter of a triangle is 50. The length of the longest side of the triangle could be

A) 15   B) 20   C) 25   D) 29

23.

24. If $x \square y$ is defined as $(x + y)^2 - 2xy$, then $5 \square 7 =$

A) 12   B) 24   C) 35   D) 74

24.

25. A square of side-length 4π has the same perimeter as a circle of diameter

A) 2   B) 4   C) 8   D) 16

25.

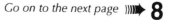

Go on to the next page)))➡ **8**

33

26. Sprinkles the dog likes to chase marching bands. When he does, he runs at 18 km per hour, which is the same as running at _?_ m per second.

    A) 5   B) 6   C) 10   D) 18

    26.

27. If the sum of 2 integers is 25, the product of the integers could not be

    A) -150   B) -30   C) 100   D) 154

    27.

28. How many of the first 1000 positive integers are multiples of both 4 and 5 but not of 6?

    A) 34   B) 42   C) 50   D) 58

    28.

29. $\frac{3}{5} : 6 = 8 : \underline{?}$

    A) $\frac{20}{9}$ B) $\frac{9}{5}$ C) 24   D) 80

    29.

30. If the average of three positive integers is 5, the greatest possible value of the sum of the squares of the three integers is

    A) 107   B) 149   C) 171   D) 197

    30.

31. After a long walk yesterday, Cody wants to go 50% farther today in half as much time. What percent faster will she have to walk today than she did yesterday to meet her goal?

    A) 200%   B) 300%   C) 400%   D) 500%

    31.

32. What is the greatest prime factor of $9^{18} - 3^{32}$?

    A) 5   B) 17   C) 19   D) 31

    32.

33. How many factors of $3 \times 6 \times 9 \times 12 \times 15 \times 18$ are greater than 1 and are the square of an integer?

    A) 15   B) 14   C) 7   D) 6

    33.

34. Each time Bette fills out a form, she marks *just one* box: A, B, or C. If she checks boxes at random, the probability that in filling out 3 such forms she will mark one each of A, B, and C is

    A) $\frac{1}{4}$ B) $\frac{1}{3}$ C) $\frac{2}{9}$ D) $\frac{3}{10}$

    34.

35. In the sequence 105, 107, 112, 114, ..., every number besides 105 and 107 is 7 greater than an earlier number. Which of the following may appear in this sequence?

    A) 1296   B) 1648   C) 2137   D) 2818

    35.

The end of the contest ✍ **8**

Visit our Web site at http://www.mathleague.com
Solutions on Page 99 • Answers on Page 144

MATH LEAGUE PRESS

P.O. Box 17, Tenafly, New Jersey 07670-0017

2013-2014 Annual 8th Grade Contest

Tuesday, February 18 or 25, 2014

8

Instructions

- **Time** Do *not* open this booklet until you are told by your teacher to begin. You might be *unable* to finish all 35 questions in the 30 minutes allowed.

- **Scores** Please remember that *this is a contest, and not a test*—there is no "passing" or "failing" score. Few students score as high as 28 points (80% correct). Students with half that, 14 points, *should be commended!*

- **Format, Point Value, & Eligibility** Every answer is an A, B, C, or D. Write answers in the *Answers* column. A correct answer is worth 1 point. Unanswered questions get no credit. You **may** use a calculator.

1. The number of kilometers Skip ran is equal to the product of two odd integers. Skip may have run __?__ kilometers.

   A) 10   B) 11   C) 12   D) 14

   1.

2. $250 + 450 + 650 + 850 = 450 + 650 + 850 +$ __?__

   A) 50   B) 250   C) 550   D) 1050

   2.

3. The reciprocal of 2 plus the reciprocal of 8 equals five times the reciprocal of

   A) 2   B) 6   C) 8   D) 10

   3.

4. What is 0.0449 rounded to the nearest hundredth?

   A) 0.04   B) 0.045   C) 0.05   D) 0.055

   4.

5. If the two largest angles of a triangle are of equal degree measure, the triangle *cannot* be what kind of triangle?

   A) isosceles   B) equilateral   C) acute   D) right

   5.

6. $\dfrac{6}{10} = \dfrac{?}{15}$

   A) 9   B) 11   C) 12   D) 18

   6.

7. I have equal numbers of nickels, dimes, and quarters. If these coins have a total value less than $10, I have at most __?__ of each coin.

   A) 20   B) 24   C) 25   D) 29

   7.

8. What time is it ten hours after 10 A.M.?

   A) 8 A.M.   B) 10 A.M.   C) 6 P.M.   D) 8 P.M.

   8.

9. The product of the three smallest prime numbers divided by the sum of these three prime numbers is

   A) $\dfrac{6}{5}$ B) 1   C) $\dfrac{5}{3}$ D) 3

   9.

10. Jorge rang his bell once on Sunday, twice on Monday, and so on. Each day he rang twice as many times as he did the day before. He first rang more than 1000 times in a single day on a

    A) Friday   B) Sunday   C) Tuesday   D) Wednesday

    10.

11. The ratio of boys to girls in class is 4:5, and there are 60 girls. There are __?__ more girls than boys.

    A) 12   B) 15   C) 18   D) 21

    11.

12. A square with a perimeter of 64 has an area of

    A) 32   B) 64   C) 144   D) 256

    12.

Go on to the next page ⟩⟩⟩➡ **8**

13. If $\frac{1}{6}$ the number of stretches Sue and Lou do is 5 less than $\frac{1}{4}$ the number they do, how many stretches do they do?

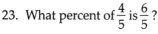

  A) 120   B) 60   C) 29   D) 24

13.

14. Of the following, which has the greatest value: $2^{5000}, 3^{4000}, 4^{3000},$ or 5^{2000}?

  A) 2^{5000} B) 3^{4000} C) 4^{3000} D) 5^{2000}

14.

15. $5 \times 5 + 5 \div 5 - 5 = 5 - 5 \div 5 + 5 \times 5 - \underline{\ ?\ }$

  A) 0   B) 8   C) 15   D) 24

15.

16. 0.25% of 50% of 1600 =

  A) 2   B) 40   C) 100   D) 200

16.

17. The sum of two primes is prime. One of the two primes added must be

  A) 2   B) 3   C) 5   D) 7

17.

18. If 2 sides of an isosceles triangle have length 10 and 25, its perimeter is

  A) 45   B) 60   C) 70   D) 75

18.

19. I interviewed 7 actors for the roles of Hamlet and Othello. In how many different ways can I cast these two roles from these 7 actors?

  A) 13   B) 21   C) 42   D) 49

19.

20. Two lines cross, creating four angles. If two of the angles measure 60° each, then each of the two remaining angles measures

  A) 40°   B) 60°   C) 90°   D) 120°

20.

21. A small model of Jeannie's big bottle is made. Every 1 mm on the model represents 2 cm on the big bottle. If the big bottle is 2 m tall, the model is _?_ tall.

  A) 0.02 m   B) 0.1 m   C) 0.2 m   D) 1 m

21.

22. Which of the following is not a possible probability?

  A) 0.02   B) $\frac{3}{\pi}$ C) $\frac{3}{5}$ D) $\frac{7}{6}$

22.

23. What percent of $\frac{4}{5}$ is $\frac{6}{5}$?

  A) 150%   B) 80%   C) 66%   D) 40%

23.

24. If 36 splorks = 24 splikes, then 36 splikes = _?_ splorks.

  A) 12   B) 24   C) 48   D) 54

24.

25. The sum of 8 consecutive even integers, each greater than 30, is at least

  A) 240   B) 256   C) 276   D) 312

25.

Go on to the next page))) **8**

26. Eli can't figure out how that desk got under his elephant! If the elephant's weight in kg is a power of 8, the ones digit of the weight in kg could be

A) 0   B) 3   C) 6   D) 9

26. _____

27. If I multiply a divisor of 24 by a divisor of 35, the product could *not* be

A) 1   B) 42   C) 56   D) 66

27. _____

28. A rectangle is 4 times as long as it is wide. If its perimeter is 40, what is its area?

A) 100   B) 64   C) 40   D) 24

28. _____

29. Sophia's average score after 6 tests was 82. Her average score on the 7th and 8th tests was a 98. What is her average score for all 8 tests?

A) 86   B) 88   C) 90   D) 94

29. _____

30. How many integers from 1 through 1000 have 0 as at least one digit?

A) 162   B) 171   C) 180   D) 181

30. _____

31. Five distinct points were chosen on a circle and every possible pair of these points was connected by a line segment. The interior of the circle is divided into _?_ regions.

A) 18   B) 16   C) 15   D) 11

31. _____

32. When I divide one integer by another, the quotient is 27.18. Which of the following could be the remainder when I do the same division?

A) 12   B) 24   C) 36   D) 48

32. _____

33. The least integer greater than 1 that leaves a remainder of 1 when divided by each integer 2, 3, 4, 5, 6, 7, 8, and 9 is between

A) 2 and 1000   B) 1000 and 2000 C) 2000 and 3000 D) 3000 and 4000

33. _____

34. Mr. Zilch's pocket just became empty. Nine minutes ago, his pocket was exactly half full. He was putting coins into it at a rate that would have filled his empty pocket in 36 minutes. A hole in his pocket was leaking coins at a rate that would have emptied his full pocket in _?_ minutes.

A) 12   B) 18   C) 36   D) 72

34. _____

35. We mixed some of my ore that is 10% gold with some of your ore that is 15% gold. We got 1.8 kg of ore that contained 228 g of pure gold. The mix included how many grams of my ore?

A) 820   B) 840   C) 880   D) 960

35. _____

The end of the contest **8**

/M|A\
\T|H/

MATH LEAGUE PRESS

P.O. Box 17, Tenafly, New Jersey 07670-0017

2014-2015 Annual 8th Grade Contest

Tuesday, February 17 or 24, 2015

8

Instructions

- **Time** Do *not* open this booklet until you are told by your teacher to begin. You might be *unable* to finish all 35 questions in the 30 minutes allowed.

- **Scores** Please remember that *this is a contest, and not a test*—there is no "passing" or "failing" score. Few students score as high as 28 points (80% correct). Students with half that, 14 points, *should be commended!*

- **Format, Point Value, & Eligibility** Every answer is an A, B, C, or D. Write answers in the *Answers* column. A correct answer is worth 1 point. Unanswered questions get no credit. You **may** use a calculator.

1. $2014 + 2015 = 1014 + 1015 + \underline{\ ?\ }$ A) 200 $\quad$ B) 1000 $\quad$ C) 1200 $\quad$ D) 2000	1.
2. Sam has demolished a number of houses equal to the product of two consecutive integers. He may have demolished $\underline{\ ?\ }$ houses. A) 54 $\quad$ B) 63 $\quad$ C) 72 $\quad$ D) 81	2.
3. The product of 8 000 000 000 and 5 000 000 000 has $\underline{\ ?\ }$ digits. A) 20 $\quad$ B) 19 $\quad$ C) 11 $\quad$ D) 10	3.
4. The sum of the largest odd factor of 380 and the largest even factor of 380 is A) 759 $\quad$ B) 475 $\quad$ C) 285 $\quad$ D) 171	4.
5. A square has a perimeter that is the square of an integer. The length of one side of the square could be A) 1 $\quad$ B) 2 $\quad$ C) 3 $\quad$ D) 5	5.
6. My sandwich cost 10 quarters, 10 dimes, and 10 nickels, and I paid for it with a \$20 bill. How much change did I get back? A) \$8.00 $\quad$ B) \$10.00 $\quad$ C) \$12.00 $\quad$ D) \$16.00	6.
7. When the time is 600 seconds after midnight, the time is A) 12:10 P.M. $\quad$ B) 10:00 P.M. $\quad$ C) 12:10 A.M. $\quad$ D) 10:00 A.M.	7.
8. $32 \div 2 \times 4 - 6 =$ A) -8 $\quad$ B) -2 $\quad$ C) 16 $\quad$ D) 58	8.
9. The sum of the first 8 prime numbers is A) 17 $\quad$ B) 59 $\quad$ C) 77 $\quad$ D) 89	9.
10. Deborah Harried hasn't had much free time today. She had only two breaks, each for a whole number of minutes. If the product of the two whole numbers is prime, she could have had a total of $\underline{\ ?\ }$ minutes of break time. A) 5 $\quad$ B) 12 $\quad$ C) 13 $\quad$ D) 19	10.
11. $\dfrac{5+5}{8+8} = \dfrac{5}{8} + \underline{\ ?\ }$ A) 0 $\quad$ B) $\dfrac{5}{16}$ $\quad$ C) $\dfrac{5}{8}$ $\quad$ D) 1	11.
12. The measures of two angles in a right triangle differ by 40°. What is the least possible measure of one of the angles in the triangle? A) 10° $\quad$ B) 25° $\quad$ C) 40° $\quad$ D) 50°	12.

Go on to the next page)))) **8**

40

13. Of the following, which is least? A) -100^2 B) $(-49)^2$ C) 19^3 D) $(0.5)^4$	13.
14. Mr. Lupu cut Merino's pay by 20% last year, and then cut this lower pay by 20% last week! If Merino now earns \$640 per week, Merino's weekly pay was \$? before the cuts. A) 896.00 B) 921.60 C) 1000.00 D) 1066.67	14.
15. The average of 6 6's and 3 12's is A) 6 B) 8 C) 8.5 D) 9	15.
16. The sum of the tenths and hundreds digits of 321.123 is A) 2 B) 3 C) 4 D) 5	16.
17. What is the remainder when $7^{77} + 7^7 + 7$ is divided by 7? A) 0 B) 1 C) 3 D) 4	17.
18. $\left(-\dfrac{6}{5}\right) \times \left(-\dfrac{5}{4}\right) \times \left(-\dfrac{4}{3}\right) \times \left(-\dfrac{3}{2}\right) \times \left(-\dfrac{2}{1}\right) \times \left(-\dfrac{1}{6}\right) = \left(\dfrac{?}{720}\right)$ A) -720 B) -1 C) 1 D) 720	18.
19. The sum of a whole number and its reciprocal cannot be A) 2.0 B) 2.8 C) 4.25 D) 8.125	19.
20. Jen has a total of \$2 in pennies, nickels, dimes, and quarters. She has at least some of each type of coin. She has at most ? dimes. A) 13 B) 14 C) 15 D) 16	20.
21. Tom's average daily number of hours in the sun for the last 6 days is twice his average daily number of hours in the sun for the last 4 days. If he spent 12 hours in the sun in the last 4 days, then he spent ? hours in the sun in the last 6 days. A) 12 B) 24 C) 36 D) 48	21.
22. $20 + 40 + 60 + 80 + 100 = (4 + 8 + 12 + 16 + 20) \times$? A) 4 B) 5 C) 25 D) 5^5	22.
23. Let $x \lozenge y = (2 \times x) - y$. Then $3 \lozenge (2 \lozenge 1) =$ A) 3 B) 5 C) 7 D) 9	23.
24. Each leg of an isosceles right triangle of area 60 is as long as the side of a square with area A) 30 B) 60 C) 120 D) 225	24.
25. The product of three primes has at most ? positive divisors. A) 3 B) 6 C) 7 D) 8	25.

Go on to the next page))▶ **8**

41

26. At work I asked each person who wanted ice cream to raise a hand. If 10% of 100% of 1000% of the 30 people at work raised hands, _?_ people raised their hands. A) 3 B) 10 C) 15 D) 30	26.
27. The positive integer x has 6 whole-number factors. The product of these 6 factors is A) x^3 B) x^4 C) x^6 D) x^7	27.
28. The sum of 8 consecutive integers could be A) 0 B) 2 C) 4 D) 8	28.
29. If one-fourth of the square of an integer is less than 1, then the integer is one of exactly _?_ possibilities. A) 1 B) 2 C) 3 D) 4	29.
30. Which of the following *cannot* be the degree measures of two of the angles in a certain isosceles triangle? A) 40, 80 B) 45, 90 C) 50, 65 D) 60, 60	30.
31. The difference between two primes between 110 and 130 could be A) 2 B) 3 C) 8 D) 14	31.
32. 3×2^{96} has the same value as A) $2^{97} + 2$ B) $2^{97} + 2^{96}$ C) $6^{32} + 6^{32}$ D) 6^{96}	32.
33. I got 90% of my math test questions and 90% of my history test questions correct. If I got 18 more questions correct on my math test than on my history test, my math test had _?_ more questions than my history test. A) 18 B) 20 C) 36 D) 180	33.
34. The masked mathematician takes mere seconds to multiply every multiple of 2 from 2 to 20 by every multiple of 3 from 3 to 30. He adds all of the products, and the total is A) 18 150 B) 108 900 C) 217 800 D) 653 400	34.
35. Two lines are parallel, and each of them is marked with 5 different dots. How many triangles can be formed using these dots as vertices? A) 80 B) 90 C) 100 D) 110	35.

The end of the contest **8**

MATH LEAGUE PRESS

P.O. Box 17, Tenafly, New Jersey 07670-0017

2015-2016 Annual 8th Grade Contest

Tuesday, February 16 or 23, 2016

Instructions

8

- **Time** Do *not* open this booklet until you are told by your teacher to begin. You might be *unable* to finish all 35 questions in the 30 minutes allowed.

- **Scores** Please remember that *this is a contest, and not a test*—there is no "passing" or "failing" score. Few students score as high as 28 points (80% correct). Students with half that, 14 points, *should be commended!*

- **Format, Point Value, & Eligibility** Every answer is an A, B, C, or D. Write answers in the *Answers* column. A correct answer is worth 1 point. Unanswered questions get no credit. You **may** use a calculator.

1. The only integer between 1 and 9 that 2016 is *not* divisible by is

   A) 4 B) 5 C) 6 D) 7

   1.

2. Each of the 10 logs Wally chewed up weighed 750 grams. Wally has chewed up a total of _?_ kilograms of logs.

   A) 0.075 B) 0.75 C) 7.5 D) 75

   2.

3. $12 \div 6 + 3 \times 0 - 3 =$

   A) -3 B) -1 C) 1 D) 3

   3.

4. 20% of 0.3% of 40000 =

   A) 24 B) 240 C) 2400 D) 24000

   4.

5. If my quiz grades are 10, 20, 30, 30, 40, and 50, which of the following measurements of my quizzes is greatest?

   A) mean B) median C) range D) mode

   5.

6. Which of the following is a prime?

   A) 2016 B) 2015 C) 2013 D) 2011

   6.

7. The sum of 4 consecutive positive integers is always divisible by

   A) 2 B) 3 C) 4 D) 5

   7.

8. The greatest number of vertices of a cube that can be chosen such that no two of the chosen vertices are on the same face of the cube is

   A) 1 B) 2 C) 3 D) 4

   8.

9. If 12345 is divided by 100, the sum of the hundreds digit and the tenths digits is

   A) 3 B) 5 C) 7 D) 9

   9.

10. Bob's bricklaying crew lays 10 bricks in the first hour, and each subsequent hour they lay 10 bricks plus an additional number of bricks equal to all bricks from all prior hours. In an 8-hour work day they lay _?_ bricks.

    A) 280 B) 360 C) 1280 D) 2550

    10.

11. How many positive integer factors do 80 and 210 have in common?

    A) 2 B) 3 C) 4 D) 5

    11.

12. A ball and a bat cost $34.10 in total. If the bat costs $20 more than the ball, how much, in dollars, does the ball cost?

    A) 7.05 B) 7.10 C) 27.05 D) 27.10

    12.

Go on to the next page)))▶ **8**

13. The Cliff Club found a pot of coins with 1000 quarters, 2000 dimes, 3000 nickels, and 4000 pennies in it. The average coin in the pot is worth

    A) 3.2¢   B) 32¢   C) 6.4¢   D) 64¢

    13.

14. Which of the following is closest to 0.9^{2016}?

    A) 0   B) 0.3   C) 0.9   D) 1

    14.

15. A book had been priced at $20 before the price went up by 30% yesterday. If Jon buys the book today at a 30% discount from the new price, Jon pays

    A) $15.00   B) $18.20   C) $20.00   D) $23.80

    15.

16. In a certain obtuse triangle the measure of the smallest angle is one third the measure of the largest. The middle angle could measure

    A) 100°   B) 80°   C) 60°   D) 40°

    16.

17. A positive multiple of 2 less than 100 is chosen at random. What is the probability that it will also be a multiple of 4?

    A) $\frac{1}{4}$ B) $\frac{11}{24}$ C) $\frac{24}{49}$ D) $\frac{1}{2}$

    17.

18. The nine consecutive integers from 1 000 001 to 1 000 009 are multiplied together. What is the ones digit of this product?

    A) 0   B) 1   C) 4   D) 5

    18.

19. How many integers have reciprocals that are also integers?

    A) 0   B) 1   C) 2   D) 3

    19.

20. What is the remainder when $17^{18} + 19^{20}$ is divided by 10?

    A) 0   B) 1   C) 8   D) 9

    20.

21. At the end of each day, the amount of water in a rain barrel doubles. If the barrel is 1/64 full at the end of Day 1. It is 1/2 full at the end of Day

    A) 5   B) 6   C) 7   D) 8

    21.

22. At _?_ Dapper Dan wins the game, 159 360 seconds after midnight!

    A) 8:08 AM B) 8:16 AM C) 8:08 PM D) 8:16 PM

    22.

23. $2^3 \times 3^4 \times 5^4 = 4 \times 27 \times 125 \times$ _?_

    A) 15   B) 30   C) 60   D) 120

    23.

24. If $5^{336} \times 25^{336} \times 125^{336} = 5^x$, what is the value of x?

    A) 1008   B) 1344   C) 1680   D) 2016

    24.

25. If $x@y = xy - x - y$, what is the value of $2@(3@4)$?

    A) -1   B) 1   C) 3   D) 10

    25.

Go on to the next page ⟫⟫➡ **8**

45

26. On the 1st day Baron flies, he flies 1 m. If each day after that he flies twice as far as he had the day before, on the 17th, 18th, and 19th days Baron will fly a total of __?__ m.

    A) 7×2^{16} B) 3×2^{18} C) 2^{19} D) 2^{20}

26.

27. How many positive integers could be the length of the third side of a triangle if the other two sides have lengths 35 and 65?

    A) 29 B) 69 C) 70 D) 71

27.

28. In my garden, the ratio of peas to parsnips is 6:5, peppers to parsnips is 3:2, and potatoes to peas is 3:8, so the ratio of potatoes to peppers is

    A) 3:10 B) 4:5 C) 5:4 D) 10:3

28.

29. At a certain farm, 20 percent of the eggs laid were large, but 2 percent of the eggs that weren't large were labeled large as well. If 50 eggs were incorrectly labeled large, how many eggs were laid?

    A) 2500 B) 3125 C) 6250 D) 50 000

29.

30. If the square of a number less than zero is less than $\frac{1}{16}$, then the reciprocal of the number must be

    A) less than -4 B) between -4 and 0
    C) between 0 and 4 D) greater than 4

30.

31. If I multiply consecutive positive integers starting with 1, at least how many integers must I multiply for the product to be a multiple of 2016?

    A) 7 B) 8 C) 21 D) 63

31.

32. What is the probability that the product of a random two-digit positive integer and the next consecutive integer will be a multiple of 3?

    A) $\frac{1}{3}$ B) $\frac{1}{2}$ C) $\frac{3}{5}$ D) $\frac{2}{3}$

32.

33. A certain bridge could be built by Al in 2 years, by Barb in 3 years, or by Cy in 6 years. Working together, they can build the bridge in __?__ years.

    A) 1 B) 1.2 C) 1.6 D) 1.8

33.

34. On each bounce, the arc of Pat's path forms a semicircle of radius 10 cm with the ground. What is the area, in mm², of the semicircle?

    A) 500π B) 5000π
    C) 1000π D) $10\,000\pi$

34.

35. Four couples enter a raffle with 4 individual winners. In how many ways can the winners be selected so that they include at least one couple?

    A) 16 B) 50 C) 54 D) 60

35.

The end of the contest

Algebra Course 1 Contests

2011-2012 through 2015-2016

2011-2012 Annual Algebra Course 1 Contest

Spring, 2012

Instructions

- **Time** Do *not* open this booklet until you are told by your teacher to begin. You will have only *30 minutes* working time for this contest. You might be *unable* to finish all 30 questions in the time allowed.

- **Scores** Please remember that *this is a contest, and not a test*—there is no "passing" or "failing" score. Few students score as high as 24 points (80% correct). Students with half that, 12 points, *should be commended!*

- **Format and Point Value** This is a multiple-choice contest. Each answer is an A, B, C, or D. Write each answer in the *Answer Column* to the right of each question. A correct answer is worth 1 point. Unanswered questions receive no credit. You **may** use a calculator.

1. If $x = 2012$ and $y = 2011$, then $(x + y)(x - y) =$ A) $2012 + 2011$ B) $2012 - 2011$ C) 2012^2 D) 2011^2	1.
2. The length of my dog's rope is twice the reciprocal of $2r$. What is the length of my dog's rope in terms of r?  A) r B) $\frac{1}{r}$ C) $4r$ D) $\frac{1}{4r}$	2.
3. If two vertices of a right triangle are $(3,5)$ and $(13,5)$, the third vertex could be A) $(16,10)$ B) $(8,7)$ C) $(5,5)$ D) $(13,13)$	3.
4. What is the sum of the roots of $(x - 6)(x + 12) = 0$? A) -18 B) -6 C) 6 D) 18	4.
5. If the average of x and y is 5, then what is the value of $(x + y)^2$? A) 25 B) 50 C) 100 D) 400	5.
6. If s is the number of positive multiples of 7 that are less than 700, then the number of positive multiples of 7 that are less than 770 is A) $s + 7$ B) $s + 9$ C) $s + 10$ D) $s + 11$	6.
7. $(x + 1) - (2 - 2x) - (x - 1) + (2 + 2x) =$ A) 0 B) 2 C) $4x + 2$ D) $2x + 4$	7.
8. Divide the numerical value of a circle's area by the numerical value of its circumference. If the quotient is 4, the circle's diameter is A) 2 B) 4 C) 8 D) 16	8.
9. $\dfrac{x^3 + x^2}{x} =$ A) $2x^2$ B) $x^2 + x$ C) $x^3 + x$ D) x^4 	9.
10. Bo is trying to impress his grumpy bosses by lifting weights at his desk. He does n lifts. If $n^2 - 18n = -81$, he does __?__ lifts. A) 9 B) 18 C) 36 D) 81	10.
11. The ratio of red roses to yellow roses in my garden is 5:3. If there are 14 more red roses than yellow ones, there are __?__ red roses. A) 12 B) 17 C) 21 D) 35	11.

Go on to the next page)))➡ **A**

12. Which of the following is an equation of a line that is perpendicular to the line $2x - 3y = -9$?

A) $3x - 4y = -12$ B) $2x - 3y = 12$ C) $3x + 2y = -10$ D) $2x + 3y = 18$

12.

13. Horace Hippo is waiting for his client, Wilbur, who will arrive in h hours. If $h^2 - 2h < 15$ and h is an integer, Horace will wait at most __?__ hours.

A) 6   B) 5   C) 4   D) 3

13.

14. I have $|3x|$ pencils and you have $|-2x|$ pencils. Together we have __?__ pencils.

A) $|x|$ B) x C) $5x$ D) $5|x|$

14.

15. My age and my sister's age are the roots of $x^2 - 20x + 91 = 0$. My age and my brother's age are the roots of the equation $x^2 - 22x + 117 = 0$. The sum of my brother's age and my sister's age is

A) 16   B) 20   C) 22   D) 26

15.

16. If 3 is one solution of the equation $x^2 + 2x + c = 21$, where c is a constant, what is the other solution?

A) -5   B) -2   C) 2   D) 7

16.

17. What is the largest of 10 consecutive integers whose sum is 75?

A) 10   B) 12   C) 15   D) 17

17.

18. Which of the following lines passes through only quadrants I and II?

A) $y = x + 2$ B) $y = 2x - 1$ C) $y = 1$ D) $x = 1$

18.

19. The average of x, y, and z is 6, and the average of a, b, and c is 4. What is the value of $(x + y + z)^2 - (a + b + c)^2$?

A) 4   B) 20   C) 36   D) 180

19.

20. Bo's bosses are grumpy because they can't figure out that the least common multiple of n^2, n^4, and n^5 is

A) n^2 B) n^5 C) n^{11} D) n^{20}

20.

21. $2[2(2^3)^4]^5 \div \{2[2(2^5)^4]^3\} =$

A) 1   B) 2   C) 2^2 D) 2^3

21.

22. If x is a positive integer, then, in terms of x, the number of integers that are both less than $4x$ and greater than $2x$ is

A) x B) $2x - 1$ C) $2x$ D) $2x + 1$

22.

Go on to the next page)))⯈ A

23. Gary's get-well gift weighs k kg, where k is an integer. If k is a root of a quadratic equation, that equation could *not* be

A) $k^2 - 2k = 8$ B) $k^2 - 2k = 15$

C) $k^2 - 2k = 24$ D) $k^2 - 2k = 30$

| 23. |

24. If $\frac{4}{x} < 12$, which of the following must

always be true?

A) $x > 3$ B) $x > \frac{1}{3}$ C) $\frac{1}{x} < 3$ D) $\frac{1}{x} < \frac{1}{3}$

| 24. |

25. If $x + y = a$ and $xy = b$, then what is the value of $x^3 + y^3$ in terms of a and b?

A) $a^3 + 3ab$ B) $a^3 - 3ab$ C) $a^3 + b^3$ D) $a^3 - b^3$

| 25. |

26. If I subtract the square of one integer from the square of another integer, then the difference could be

A) 386   B) 558   C) 768   D) 970

| 26. |

27. For any positive integer n, $n!$ is the product of all positive integers less than or equal to n. If $n > 0$ and $(n!)^2 - 21(n!) - 72 = 0$, then $n =$

A) 6   B) 5   C) 4   D) 3

| 27. |

28. If $3x + 4y = 6z$ and x, y, and z are each integers, which of the following could be the value of y?

A) 285   B) 319   C) 422   D) 500

| 28. |

29. We drove from our home to the beach at 90 km/hr., and immediately returned along the same route at 110 km/hr. Our average rate for the entire trip was __?__ km/hr.

A) 98   B) 99   C) 100   D) 101

| 29. |

30. The roots of the equation $x^2 - cx + 36 = 0$ are in a 4:1 ratio. Which of the following is the product of both possible values of c?

A) -225   B) -36   C) 15   D) 120

| 30. |

The end of the contest **A**

2012-2013 Annual Algebra Course 1 Contest

Spring, 2013

Instructions

- **Time** Do *not* open this booklet until you are told by your teacher to begin. You will have only *30 minutes* working time for this contest. You might be *unable* to finish all 30 questions in the time allowed.

- **Scores** Please remember that *this is a contest, and not a test*—there is no "passing" or "failing" score. Few students score as high as 24 points (80% correct). Students with half that, 12 points, *should be commended!*

- **Format and Point Value** This is a multiple-choice contest. Each answer is an A, B, C, or D. Write each answer in the *Answer Column* to the right of each question. A correct answer is worth 1 point. Unanswered questions receive no credit. You **may** use a calculator.

1. If $x = 2013$, then $(x - 2012)^{(x - 2013)} =$ 1.

    A) 0   B) 1   C) 2   D) 10

2. If $a = 5$, then $4a^3 - 3a^2 + 2a - 1 =$ 2.

    A) 39   B) 125   C) 434   D) 586

3. Fred and Ginger danced for $\dfrac{2013}{x}$ hours   3.
   last year. If they danced for a whole
   number of hours, then x *cannot* be

    A) 3   B) 11   C) 13   D) 61

4. Which of the following is a factor   4.
   of $x^2 - 4x - 12$?

    A) $x + 2$ B) $x - 2$ C) x D) $x - 8$

5. $2^{400} + 2^{400} =$ 5.

    A) 2^{401} B) 2^{800} C) 4^{400} D) 4^{800}

6. If $\dfrac{p}{q} = \dfrac{2}{3}$, then $\dfrac{-p}{-q} =$ 6.

    A) $-\dfrac{2}{3}$ B) $\dfrac{-2}{3}$ C) $\dfrac{2}{-3}$ D) $\dfrac{2}{3}$

7. The number of 5 kg weights and 10 kg weights I have is $4w$ and $2w$,   7.
   respectively. If my weights all together weigh 200 kg, then $w =$

    A) 4   B) 5   C) 10   D) 20

8. $(3x^3 - 4x^2) + (2x^2 - 3x) - (3x^3 - 4) =$ 8.

    A) $2x^2 - 3x - 4$ B) $2x^2 - 3x + 4$ C) $-2x^2 - 3x - 4$ D) $-2x^2 - 3x + 4$

9. If $3x - 4$ is odd, then $3x + 10$ must be   9.

    A) positive   B) prime   C) odd   D) even

10. Telly the dog grabs the phone when   10.
    it rings. Yesterday it rang at 4 PM or
    later 80% of the time it rang, and it
    rang 50 times before 4 PM. The
    phone rang _?_ times yesterday.

    A) 200   B) 250   C) 300   D) 400

11. The ages of 5 sequoia trees in a forest are consecutive even integers.   11.
    If the total of the trees' ages is 4440 years, the oldest tree is _?_ old.

    A) 884 years   B) 888 years   C) 890 years   D) 892 years

Go on to the next page))))➡ **A**

12. A straight line that passes through the points (p,q) and $(2p,3q)$ must also pass through the point

    A) $(3p,4q)$ B) $(3p,5q)$ C) $(4p,6q)$ D) $(4p,8q)$

    12.

13. What is the product of all multiples of 3 between -9 and 12?

    A) -314928   B) -2916   C) 0   D) 2916

    13.

14. Of children born at the maternity ward yesterday, the ratio of boys to girls was $3x:4y$, which is also 5:6. The ratio $x:y$ is

    A) 10:9   B) 24:15   C) 15:24   D) 4:5

    14.

15. $$\frac{\left(x^{200}\right)^{400}}{\left(x^{100}\right)^{200}} =$$

    A) x^4 B) x^6 C) $x^{40\,000}$ D) $x^{60\,000}$

    15.

16. If the average of x, y, and z is 16 and the average of x and y is 12, then $z =$

    A) 4   B) 14   C) 20   D) 24

    16.

17. If n is a prime > 5, the least common multiple of $6n^8$ and $10n^{12}$ is

    A) $2n^8$ B) $30n^{12}$ C) $30n^{24}$ D) $60n^{96}$

    17.

18. A square is inscribed in a circle. If the perimeter of the square region is 64, what is the area of the circle?

    A) 16π B) 32π C) 64π D) 128π

    18.

19. If $x - y = 3$ and $x^2 + y^2 = 485$ then $xy =$

    A) 162   B) 238   C) 482   D) 3880

    19.

20. Gilda the guide has a lucky number that is the sum of all the roots of $(x-1)(x+2)(x-3) \times \ldots \times (x-19)(x+20)(x-21) = 0$. Gilda's lucky number is

    A) 10   B) 11   C) 21   D) 31

    20.

21. $|4x| + 4|-x| =$

    A) 0   B) 8   C) $8|x|$ D) $4|4x|$

    21.

22. $\sqrt{36^{64}} =$

    A) 6^8 B) 6^{32} C) 36^8 D) 36^{32}

    22.

Go on to the next page))))⟶ **A**

23. If $(x-2)^2 = 1600$, which of the following could be the value of $x-4$?   23.

    A) -42   B) -34   C) 34   D) 36

24. If x is a positive integer, and the product of all integers from 1 to x, inclusive, is a multiple of 260, then the least possible value of x is   24.

    A) 10   B) 13   C) 26   D) 30

25. Don Q rides at $3r$ kph for the first 60 km of a trip, and then rides at $6r$ kph for the next 60 km. What is his average speed for the entire trip?   25.

    A) $4r$ B) $4.5r$ C) $5r$ D) $5.5r$

26. If I reverse the digits of a two-digit positive integer and subtract the resulting integer from the original integer, the difference is 36. The difference between the two digits is   26.

    A) 4   B) 6   C) 8   D) 9

27. My sister has s dollars, and I have d dollars more than she has. If together we have a total of t dollars, which of the following is equivalent to s?   27.

    A) $t-2d$ B) $\dfrac{t}{2}-d$ C) $t-\dfrac{d}{2}$ D) $\dfrac{t-d}{2}$

28. If x is an integer, which of the following must be divisible by 3?   28.

    A) $x(x-3)(x-6)$ B) $x(x+3)(x-3)$ C) $x(x+7)(x-2)$ D) $x(x+1)(x-1)$

29. If $x \neq 0$ or 1, and each x in the expression $\dfrac{2x+1}{3x-3}$ is replaced by $\dfrac{4}{x}$, then the resulting expression is equivalent to   29.

    A) $\dfrac{2x+1}{3x-3}$ B) $\dfrac{3x-3}{2x+1}$ C) $\dfrac{8+x}{12-3x}$ D) $\dfrac{12x-3}{8x+1}$

30. The number of passengers in my car is the same as the number of integers less than 8 that satisfy   30.

$$\dfrac{(x+3)(x+4)}{x-5} \geq 0.$$

    My car has __?__ passengers.

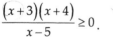

    A) 2   B) 3   C) 4   D) 5

The end of the contest 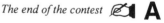 **A**

Visit our Web site at http://www.mathleague.com
Solutions on Page 121 • Answers on Page 149

2013-2014 Annual Algebra Course 1 Contest

Spring, 2014

Instructions

- **Time** Do *not* open this booklet until you are told by your teacher to begin. You will have only *30 minutes* working time for this contest. You might be *unable* to finish all 30 questions in the time allowed.

- **Scores** Please remember that *this is a contest, and not a test*—there is no "passing" or "failing" score. Few students score as high as 24 points (80% correct). Students with half that, 12 points, *should be commended!*

- **Format and Point Value** This is a multiple-choice contest. Each answer is an A, B, C, or D. Write each answer in the *Answer Column* to the right of each question. A correct answer is worth 1 point. Unanswered questions receive no credit. You **may** use a calculator.

1. If $x = 3$, then $2014x^2 - 2014x + 2014 =$

   A) 2014   B) 2014×3 C) 2014×6 D) 2014×7

   1.

2. If x is an integer, then the least integral value of $\dfrac{6}{x}$ is

   A) -6   B) -3   C) -1   D) 1

   2.

3. Max Peters completed a series of smiley face paintings. He painted p faces, each of which has 2 eyes, and one additional face with only one eye. He painted a total of _?_ eyes.

   A) $p^2 + 1$ B) $2(p + 1)$ C) $2p + 1$ D) $p + 3$

   3.

4. $(200^8)(200^9)(200^0) =$

   A) 200^{72} B) 200^{17} C) 200^0 D) 0

   4.

5. If $x^2 + xy = 20$ and $x + y = 10$, then $x =$

   A) 2   B) 5   C) 10   D) 30

   5.

6. The least common multiple of 24 and 48 is

   A) 2   B) 48   C) 96   D) 1152

   6.

7. The reciprocal of $\sqrt{3}$ is

   A) $\sqrt{3}$ B) 3   C) $\dfrac{\sqrt{3}}{3}$ D) $\dfrac{3}{\sqrt{3}}$

   7.

8. If exactly 25% of the students in my class are wearing boots, then the ratio of students wearing boots to students not wearing boots is

   A) 25:100   B) 75:100   C) 1:4   D) 1:3

   8.

9. How many different positive integers satisfy $|x - 5| < 3$?

   A) 5   B) 7   C) 8   D) 10

   9.

10. Mr. Rorke flies his plane to a private island in $x - 20$ minutes and flies back in $x - 10$ minutes. Both flights together take a total of 76 minutes. How long would a flight of $x - 15$ minutes take?

    A) 38   B) 53   C) 61   D) 400

    10.

11. What is the sum of the roots of $x^2 - 6x - 432 = 0$?

    A) 2   B) 6   C) 18   D) 42

    11.

Go on to the next page)))➤ **A**

12. The product of the slopes of two perpendicular lines may equal A) 1 B) 4 C) -1 D) -4	12.
13. When I expand the product $(x-2)(x-1)(x-0)(x+1)(x+2)$ and combine all like terms, my polynomial has exactly how many terms? A) 6 B) 5 C) 4 D) 3	13.
14. The Fergusons are counting pairs of lovebirds from a hot air balloon. Over 5 days they see totals of n, $n+1$, $n+2$, $n+3$, and $n+4$ pairs, for a total of 360 birds. The value of n is A) 34 B) 35 C) 70 D) 140 	14.
15. Speedy the snail moves x cm per hour. How many cm does Speedy move in $10y$ minutes? A) $\dfrac{x}{600y}$ B) $6xy$ C) $\dfrac{xy}{6}$ D) $\dfrac{600y}{x}$	15.
16. If the x- and y-intercepts of a line have equal non-zero values, then the slope of the line must be A) 0 B) even C) positive D) negative	16.
17. If $x \blacklozenge y = (x+y)^2 - xy$, then what is the value of $4 \blacklozenge 2$? A) 16 B) 28 C) 32 D) 36	17.
18. A square of side-length π has the same area as a circle of radius A) 1 B) $\sqrt{\pi}$ C) π D) π^2	18.
19. If x is an integer, which of the following must be divisible by 3? A) $(x+1)(x+2)(x+4)$ B) $(x+2)(x+4)(x+5)$ C) $(x+3)(x+4)(x+6)$ D) $(x+4)(x+6)(x+8)$	19.
20. Patches the clown has 120 balloons, of which 5% are blue. If he lets 90 of the balloons go but keeps all the blue ones, then __?__ of the remaining balloons will be blue. A) 15% B) 20% C) 25% D) 30% 	20.
21. If $x^{-1} = -\dfrac{1}{4}$, then $x^{-2} =$ A) $-\dfrac{1}{2}$ B) $-\dfrac{1}{16}$ C) $\dfrac{1}{16}$ D) $\dfrac{1}{2}$ 	21.
22. If $(n-1)^2 = 81$, then __?__ could be the value of $n-4$. A) -14 B) -12 C) -10 D) -8	22.

Go on to the next page ⟫➡ **A**

23. What is the x-intercept of a line that passes through the points (2, 2) and (-4,4)?

23.

A) (0,-8)   B) (8,0)   C) $(\frac{8}{3},0)$ D) $(0,-\frac{8}{3})$

24. Points P, Q, R, and S lie on a straight line, in that order. Q is exactly halfway between P and S, and R is exactly halfway between Q and S. If the distance from Q to R is x cm and the distance from P to Q is $4x - 6$ cm, what is the distance from P to S?

24.

A) 2 cm   B) 3 cm   C) 6 cm   D) 12 cm

25. Detective Marlon Phillow is on the case, detecting how many students are in his science class. Of two science classes at the school, his class had an average score of 82 on the final exam, the other class had an average of 86, and both classes combined had an average of 85. The other class has 60 students, so Marlon's class has __?__ students.

25.

A) 20   B) 30   C) 40   D) 45

26. If x and y are primes and $\sqrt{3 \times 5} \times \sqrt{5 \times 7} \times \sqrt{xy}$ is a rational number, then $x + y$ must equal

26.

A) 10   B) 13   C) 18   D) 21

27. If $4^{31} \times 5^{61} = 2 \times 10^x$, then $x =$

27.

A) 30   B) 31   C) 60   D) 61

28. When 7^x is divided by 10 the remainder is 1. Of the following, which could be the value of x?

28.

A) 21   B) 22   C) 24   D) 25

29. $3^{100} + 3^{100} + 3^{100} + 3^{101} + 3^{101} + 3^{102} + 3^{102} + 3^{103} + 3^{103} =$

29.

A) 3^{104} B) 3^{105} C) 3^{110} D) 3^{910}

30. A hot dog eating champion had an amazing day and set a new world record by eating x hot dogs in ten minutes. If x is the only solution to $2x^2 - bx + 9800 = 0$, then what is the value of b?

30.

A) -140   B) 70   C) 280   D) 490

The end of the contest **A**

2014-2015 Annual Algebra Course 1 Contest

Spring, 2015

Instructions

- **Time** Do *not* open this booklet until you are told by your teacher to begin. You will have only *30 minutes* working time for this contest. You might be *unable* to finish all 30 questions in the time allowed.

- **Scores** Please remember that *this is a contest, and not a test*—there is no "passing" or "failing" score. Few students score as high as 24 points (80% correct). Students with half that, 12 points, *should be commended!*

- **Format and Point Value** This is a multiple-choice contest. Each answer is an A, B, C, or D. Write each answer in the *Answer Column* to the right of each question. A correct answer is worth 1 point. Unanswered questions receive no credit. You **may** use a calculator.

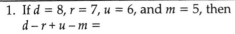

1. If $d = 8, r = 7, u = 6$, and $m = 5$, then
   $d - r + u - m =$

   A) 2   B) 3   C) 4   D) 5

   1.

2. If $x = -1$, which of the following has the greatest value?

   A) $x^3 + 1$ B) $x^2 + 1$ C) $x + 1$ D) 1

   2.

3. $x + 2 + 3x + 4 + 5x + 6 =$

   A) $3x + 21$ B) $7x + 8$ C) $8x + 10$ D) $9x + 12$

   3.

4. $(t - 3)(t - 3)(t + 3)(t + 3) =$

   A) $t^4 + 81$ B) $t^4 - 81$ C) $(t^2 - 9)^2$ D) $(t^2 + 9)^2$

   4.

5. Which of the following is divisible by $x + 4$?

   A) $x^2 + 16$ B) $x^3 + 64$ C) $x^4 - 32$ D) $x^4 + 16$

   5.

6. $(a + 4)(a - 3) - (a - 3)(a + 2) = (a - 3) \times (\underline{\ ?\ })$

   A) 2   B) 6   C) $2a + 2$ D) $2a + 6$

   6.

7. If $n = 50$, then $(n - 1)(n - 2)(n - 3)(n - 4) \dots (n - 49)(n - 50) =$

   A) 50!   B) 49!   C) 25^{25} D) 0

   7.

8. If $x + y = 10$ and $x^2 + y^2 = 20$, then $xy =$

   A) 2   B) 30   C) 40   D) 80

   8.

9. If $x \neq 0$, $x\%$ of $\dfrac{100}{x} =$

   A) 1   B) x C) 100   D) $100x$

   9.

10. Everyone was sad to wave goodbye to the last math contest of the year. There were $4c$ people crying and $7d$ people who weren't. If exactly half the people were crying, then $c : d =$

    A) 4:7 B) 4:11 C) 7:4 D) 11:4

    10.

11. $|2 - x^2| =$

    A) $|2 + x^2|$ B) $|x^2 - 2|$ C) $2 + x^2$ D) $x^2 - 2$

    11.

12. Which of the following has no real solution?

    A) $x^2 - 1 = 0$ B) $x^3 + 1 = 0$ C) $x^4 - 1 = 0$ D) $x^4 + 1 = 0$

    12.

Go on to the next page)))⟩ **A**

13. If two sides of a rectangle are $\sqrt{8}$ and $\sqrt{9}$, then the perimeter of the rectangle is

 A) $6\sqrt{2}$ B) $6+4\sqrt{2}$ C) $\sqrt{17}$ D) $\sqrt{89}$

13.

14. $(x-2)(x-1)(x+1)(x+2) = (x^2 + x - 2) \times (\underline{\ ?\ })$

 A) $x^2 + x - 2$ B) $x^2 + x + 2$ C) $x^2 - x + 2$ D) $x^2 - x - 2$

14.

15. Every time I ask my sister what line she graphed, she shushes me! I can see that her line is parallel to my line, though. If my line is $26x + 36y = 46$, then my sister's line could be

 A) $36x + 46y = 56$ B) $52x + 54y = 56$
 C) $39x + 54y = 23$ D) $13x + 36y = 23$

15.

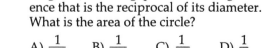

16. My sister is an odd number of years old, and so am I. The average of our ages in years must be what kind of number?

 A) odd   B) even   C) prime   D) whole

16.

17. If $x \neq 0$ or -1, $\left(\dfrac{1}{x^2} + \dfrac{1}{x^3} \right) \div (x+1) =$

 A) $\dfrac{1}{x^3}$ B) x^3 C) $\dfrac{1}{x^2}$ D) x^2

17.

18. How many integers $x < 2015$ are there such that $x + 2015 > 0$?

 A) 2014   B) 4028   C) 4029   D) 4030

18.

19. Yesterday I drove 80 km per hour for 30 minutes. Today I will drive 10 km more than yesterday, but it will take me 20 minutes longer. What will be my average speed today in km/hr?

 A) 40   B) 60   C) 70   D) 100

19.

20. If $5^{41} \times 4^{21} = 2 \times 10^x$, what is the value of x?

 A) 11   B) 20   C) 21   D) 41

20.

21. Meg loves her megaphone! The large circular end has a circumference that is the reciprocal of its diameter. What is the area of the circle?

 A) $\dfrac{1}{4\pi}$ B) $\dfrac{1}{2\pi}$ C) $\dfrac{1}{4}$ D) $\dfrac{1}{2}$

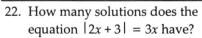

21.

22. How many solutions does the equation $|2x + 3| = 3x$ have?

 A) 0   B) 1   C) 2   D) 4

22.

Go on to the next page))))➡

23. If $y = 1 - x$, which of the following is true for all values of x? | 23.

 A) $(1 - x)^2 = (1 - y)^2$ B) $(1 - x)^2 x^2 = (1 - y)^2 y^2$

 C) $x^2 - (1 - x)^2 = y^2 - (1 - y)^2$ D) $(1 - x)^2 (1 + x)^2 = (1 - y)^2 (1 + y)^2$

24. Lee the crow ate a grams of feed that was 1% seed, b grams of feed that was 2% seed, and c grams of feed that was 3% seed. If combined, all the feed he ate was 1.5% seed. What is a in terms of b and c? | 24.

 A) $b + 3c$ B) $3b + c$ C) $2b + 3c$ D) $3b + 2c$

25. If $x < 0$ and $x^2 < 0.01$, then x^{-1} must be | 25.

 A) less than -10 B) between −0.1 and 0
 C) between 0 and 0.1 D) greater than 10

26. At 9:00 A.M., the ratio of red to black cars in a parking lot was 1 to 5. An hour later the number of red cars had increased by 2, the number of black cars had decreased by 5, and the ratio of red to black cars was 1 to 4. How many black cars were in the lot at 10:00 A.M.? | 26.

 A) 13 B) 15 C) 60 D) 65

27. If $x \ne 1$ and $x \ne -1$, then $\dfrac{4x^3(x^2 - 1) - x^2 + 1}{(x + 1)(x - 1)} =$ | 27.

 A) $x^2 - 1$ B) $x^2 + 1$ C) $4x^2 + 1$ D) $4x^3 - 1$

28. The Camps are driving at a constant rate. At noon they had driven 300 km. At 3:30 P.M. they had driven 50% further than they had driven by 1:30 P.M. What is their constant rate in km/hr? | 28.

 A) 150 B) 120 C) 100 D) 90

29. The letters in DIGITS can be arranged in how many orders without adjacent I's? | 29.

 A) 240 B) 355 C) 600 D) 715

30. Al, Bea, and Cal each paint at constant rates, and together they are painting a house. Al and Bea together could do the job in 12 hours; Al and Cal could do it in 15, and Bea and Cal could do it in 20. How many hours will it take all three working together to paint the house? | 30.

 A) 8.5 B) 9 C) 10 D) 10.5

The end of the contest **A**

2015-2016 Annual Algebra Course 1 Contest

Spring, 2016

Instructions

- **Time** Do *not* open this booklet until you are told by your teacher to begin. You will have only *30 minutes* working time for this contest. You might be *unable* to finish all 30 questions in the time allowed.

- **Scores** Please remember that *this is a contest, and not a test*—there is no "passing" or "failing" score. Few students score as high as 24 points (80% correct). Students with half that, 12 points, *should be commended!*

- **Format and Point Value** This is a multiple-choice contest. Each answer is an A, B, C, or D. Write each answer in the *Answer Column* to the right of each question. A correct answer is worth 1 point. Unanswered questions receive no credit. You **may** use a calculator.

1. The sum of the cubes of the digits of 2016 equals the sum of the cubes of the digits of

    A) 106　　B) 162　　　C) 201　　　D) 620

    1.

2. The gym charges $50 for a one-time registration fee and $3 for each visit. If Tina registers and then visits the gym n times, she will pay a total of __?__ dollars.

    A) 53　　　B) $50n + 3$　　C) $53n$　　　D) $3n + 50$

    2.

3. If $m = 2$, $a = 0$, $t = 1$, and $h = 6$, then $m^a \times t^h =$

    A) 0　　　B) 1　　　　C) 2　　　　D) 6

    3.

4. Which of the following is positive for all real numbers x?

    A) $x + 1$　　　B) $x^2 + 1$　　　C) $x^3 + 1$　　　D) x^{100}

    4.

5. $(a - 7)^2 - (a - 3)(a - 11) =$

    A) 16　　　　B) $4a + 4$　　　C) $16a - 16$　　　D) $a^2 + 4a + 4$

    5.

6. If $\sqrt{1} + \sqrt{4} + \sqrt{9} + \sqrt{16} + \sqrt{25} = \sqrt{x}$, $x =$

    A) 15　　　　B) 20　　　　C) 225　　　　D) 400

    6.

7. $(x - 6)(x + 6)(x^2 - 49)(x^2 + 49) = 0$ has __?__ real solutions.

    A) 2　　　　B) 3　　　　C) 4　　　　D) 6

    7.

8. If 25% of y is equal to 400% of x, then $y =$

    A) $2x$　　　B) $4x$　　　　C) $8x$　　　　D) $16x$

    8.

9. Baking one cake requires 3 cups of flour and 5 cups of sugar. One pie requires 4 cups of flour and 2 cups of sugar. If I use exactly 54 cups of flour and 48 cups of sugar to make cakes and pies, how many cakes will I make?

    A) 6　　B) 7　　　C) 8　　　D) 9

    9.

10. If $x - y = 5$ and $x + y = 30$, then $x^2 - y^2 =$

    A) 35　　B) -35　　　C) 150　　　D) -150

    10.

11. $(x^6)^5 \times (x^{10})^2 =$

    A) x^{23}　　B) x^{50}　　　C) x^{60}　　　D) x^{600}

    11.

12. If $x > 5$, then $|5 - x| + |x - 5| =$

    A) 0　　　　B) 10　　　C) $2(5 - x)$　　　D) $2(x - 5)$

    12.

Go on to the next page))))▶ A

13. Which of the following lines has a positive slope?

A) $y = -3x + 5$ B) $x = -3y + 5$ C) $-y - 3 = -x$ D) $3x + 4y = 5$

13.

14. Jackie is tired of carrying a huge drum in band! She wants to switch to playing the triangle, so she studies triangles. If a triangle has a base of $\sqrt{8}$ and a height of $\sqrt{18}$, what is the area of the triangle?

A) 3   B) 6   C) 12   D) 144

14.

15. Lee tried to trick her friend by pretending she has ESP. She asked Mo to pick any non-zero number x, square it, subtract x from the square, divide by x, and finally subtract x. Lee knew Mo's final answer because she knew that the final difference is always

A) -1   B) 1   C) x D) $-x$

15.

16. If $f(n) = (n-1)(n-2)(n-3) \ldots (n-98)(n-99)$, then $f(-1) =$

A) 100!   B) -100!   C) 101!   D) -101!

16.

17. If $x \neq -3$ or -4, then $\left(\dfrac{1}{x+3} + \dfrac{1}{x+4}\right)(x^2 + 7x + 12) = ?$

A) 7   B) $2x + 3$ C) $2x + 4$ D) $2x + 7$

17.

18. If $x/5 = y/6 = z/7$, then $x : y : z =$

A) 7:6:5   B) 1/5:1/6:1/7   C) 5:6:7   D) 1/7:1/6:1/5

18.

19. What is the sum of the reciprocals of two real numbers whose sum is 60 and whose product is 15?

A) 4   B) 1/4   C) 6   D) 1/6

19.

20. Andrew Giant drives from home to work at a speed of 30 m/s, then back from work to home along the same route at 20 m/s. His average speed for the round trip is

A) 24 m/s B) 25 m/s C) 26 m/s D) 27 m/s

20.

21. The radius of circle A is twice that of circle B. The radius of circle B is twice that of circle C. The radius of circle C is twice that of circle D. The area of circle A is __?__ times the area of circle D.

A) 8   B) 16   C) 64   D) 256

21.

22. For what integer n does $x \times x^2 \times x^3 \times \ldots \times x^n = x^{2016}$?

A) 62   B) 63   C) 64   D) 65

22.

Go on to the next page))))⟩ **A**

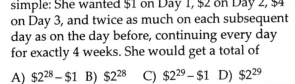

23. Jean found a Genie in a teapot! Her first wish was simple: She wanted $1 on Day 1, $2 on Day 2, $4 on Day 3, and twice as much on each subsequent day as on the day before, continuing every day for exactly 4 weeks. She would get a total of

A) $2^{28} – $1   B) $2^{28}   C) $2^{29} – $1   D) $2^{29}

23.

24. If $a(a - 1) = b(b - 1)$ and $a \neq b$, then $a =$

A) b B) $-b$ C) $b - 1$ D) $1 - b$

24.

25. How many **integers** satisfy $30 < x^2 + 7 < 300$?

A) 12   B) 13   C) 24   D) 26

25.

26. The product of 2016 different primes has ? positive divisors.

A) 2017   B) 2018   C) 2^{2016} D) 2^{2017}

26.

27. When I decrease the numerator of a fraction by 1, the new fraction is equal to 3/5. If I increase the denominator of the original fraction by 22, the new fraction is equal to 1/2. If I increase both the numerator and the denominator of the original fraction by 5, the new fraction is equal to

A) 22/35   B) 31/50   C) 36/73   D) 56/79

27.

28. Mr. Bingo has a box of colored balls, half of which are red. He starts randomly removing them from the box one at a time, without replacing them. If the probability that the first 2 balls he chooses are red is 9/38, there were ? red balls in the box before he began.

A) 10   B) 20   C) 22   D) 24

28.

29. At a certain grocery store, the cost of 5 stalks of broccoli, 4 bananas, and 8 oranges is $5.60. The cost of 7 stalks of broccoli, 3 bananas, and 10 oranges is $7.00. What is the cost of 3 stalks of broccoli, 5 bananas, and 6 oranges?

A) $1.40   B) $2.80   C) $4.20   D) $5.60

29.

30. Al, Barb, Cy, Di, Ed, Fred, and Greg stand in a straight line. If Al must stand next to Barb and Cy must stand next to Di, in how many ways can these seven people line up?

A) 240   B) 480   C) 1260   D) 5040

30.

The end of the contest **A**

Detailed Solutions

2011-2012 through 2015-2016

7th Grade Solutions

2011-2012 through 2015-2016

Information & Solutions

Tuesday, February 21 or 28, 2012

7

Contest Information

- **Solutions**   Turn the page for detailed contest solutions (written in the question boxes) and letter answers (written in the *Answer Column* to the right of each question).

- **Scores**   Please remember that *this is a contest, and not a test*—there is no "passing" or "failing" score. Few students score as high as 28 points (80% correct); students with half that, 14 points, *deserve commendation!*

- **Answers and Rating Scales**   Turn to page 138 for the letter answers to each question and the rating scale for this contest.

1. $4\,024\,000 = 2 \times 2\,012\,000 = 2012 \times 2000$, so the answer is 2000.

   A) 200   B) 2000   C) 2020   D) 20000

   1.
   B

2. 5 nickels = 1 quarter and 5 dimes = 2 quarters. The total value of 5 nickels and 5 dimes = the value of 3 quarters.

   A) 3   B) 4   C) 5   D) 6

   2.
   A

3. Since the thousandths digit is a 5, 0.3456 rounds up to 0.35.

   A) 0.34   B) 0.35   C) 0.345   D) 0.346

   3.
   B

4. The divisors of 12 are 1, 2, 3, 4, 6, and 12. Their sum is 28.

   A) 0   B) 15   C) 28   D) 56

   4.
   C

5. $1^4 + 2^4 + 3^4 = 1 + 16 + 81 = 98 = 10^2 - 2$.

   A) 123^4 B) 4^4 C) 6^4 D) $10^2 - 2$

   5.
   D

6. $(\frac{1}{2} + \frac{1}{4}) \div 2 = \frac{3}{4} \div 2 = \frac{3}{8}$.

   A) $\frac{1}{8}$ B) $\frac{1}{3}$ C) $\frac{3}{8}$ D) $\frac{6}{8}$

   6.
   C

7. Billy Beaver chews up 3 pencils per minute or 60×3 pencils in 1 hr. In 2 hours he chews up 2×180 pencils.

   A) 360   B) 180   C) 90   D) 40

   7.
   A

8. Since $21 - 14 = 7$ and $34 - 27 = 7$, the missing number is $44 - 7 = 37$.

   A) 37   B) 39   C) 51   D) 79

   8.
   A

9. The sum of the lengths of any two sides of a triangle must exceed the length of the third side, so the third side's length is less than 16.

   A) 8   B) 9   C) 12   D) 16

   9.
   D

10. Since the ratio is 4:5, the number of students is a multiple of $4 + 5 = 9$.

    A) 45   B) 32   C) 24   D) 20

    10.
    A

11. My assignment is to read from page 123 through page 321. This is the same as reading from p. $(123 - 122)$ to p. $(321 - 122)$, or p. 1 to p. 199.

    A) 198   B) 199   C) 200   D) 201

    11.
    B

12. My age 2 years ago plus my age 2 years from now equals 24, twice my age now.

    A) 10   B) 12   C) 14   D) 24

    12.
    B

13. Since the page numbers are small, try the product of the first 4 primes: $2 \times 3 \times 5 \times 7 = 210$. Since this is 1 less than 211, choice D is correct.

    A) 31   B) 121   C) 129   D) 211

    13.
    D

Go on to the next page))))⮕ 7

14. Subtract multiples of $27 from $250 until the remainder is a multiple of $22. Since $6 \times \$27 = \$162$ and $\$250 - \$162 = \$88$, 6 hats have flowers.

   A) 4   B) 5   C) 6   D) 7

14. C

15. $0.20 \times \frac{2}{3} \times 0.25 \times 300 = 0.20 \times 0.25 \times 200 = 10$.

   A) 10   B) 20   C) 40   D) 50

15. A

16. $(\frac{4}{3} \div \frac{3}{4}) = (\frac{4}{3} \times \frac{4}{3}) = \frac{16}{9}$.

   A) 1   B) $\frac{16}{9}$ C) $\frac{9}{16}$ D) $\frac{3}{4}$

16. B

17. The gcd of 264 and 528 is 264. The gcd of 264 and 660 is 132.

   A) $4 < 132$ B) $66 < 132$ C) $528 = 2 \times 264$ D) $660 = 5 \times 132$

17. D

18. My dimes and nickels have a value of $1.00. If I have 8 nickels, then I have 6 dimes. The probability that I choose a nickel is 8:14 = 4:7.

   A) $\frac{1}{2}$ B) $\frac{2}{3}$ C) $\frac{4}{3}$ D) $\frac{4}{7}$

18. D

19. $((3^4)^4)^4 \div [(9^2) \times (9^2) \times (9^2)] = 3^{4 \times 4 \times 4} \div [(3^4) \times (3^4) \times (3^4)] = 3^{64} \div 3^{12} = 3^{52}$.

   A) 1   B) 3^6 C) 3^{52} D) 3^{58}

19. C

20. 10 hours after 10 A.M. is 8 P.M.; 10 minutes before that is 7:50 P.M.

   A) 7:50 P.M.   B) 9:50 P.M.   C) 11:50 P.M.   D) 4:50 A.M.

20. A

21. The circum. of the wheel is 60π cm. He travels 540π cm, so the wheel rotates $(540\pi \div 60\pi) = 9$ times.

   A) 6   B) 9   C) 12   D) 18

21. B

22. The 3 crates of apples contain as many apples as $3 \times 16 = 48$ tubs, and 48 tubs of apples contain as many apples as 12×9 bags; so 3 crates contain as many apples as 108 bags.

   A) 36   B) 72   C) 108   D) 436

22. C

23. 20% of $30 = 0.20 \times 30 = 6 = 0.40 \times 15 = 40\%$ of 15.

   A) 15   B) 50   C) 60   D) 90

23. A

24. The sum of the measures of two adjacent angles in a parallelogram is 180°. If the angles' measures were equal, they'd both be 90°.

   A) an equal   B) an odd   C) a prime   D) a greater

24. A

25. If 10 of my 42 cousins are blond and 18 of my 24 male cousins are *not* blond, then $42 - 10 - 18 = 14$ are female and not blond.

   A) 4   B) 10   C) 12   D) 14

25. D

Go on to the next page ⟫⟫➡ **7**

26. If the sum of two prime numbers is odd, one of them must be 2. Since 81 is not prime, Ira cries if he hears 83. A) 83 B) 99 C) 103 D) 109	26. A
27. 1/800 × 1/4 × 3200 = 1/3200 × 3200 = 1. A) 1 B) 10 C) 100 D) 1000	27. A
28. If the length of a rectangle is 3 times its width, then the perimeter is 8 times the width, a multiple of 8. A) 8, w = 1 B) 16, w = 2 C) 32, w = 4 D) 44	28. D
29. 1 × 2 × 3 × ... × 18 × 19 × 20 is divisible by 5 × 7 × 11. A) 23 B) 121 C) 385 D) 580	29. C
30. Let's use the answer choices. For choice A, the average is (6×15°+ 2×40°)÷8 ≠ 20°; for B, the average is (8×15°+2×40°)÷10 = 20°; for C, it's (10×15°+2×40°)÷12 ≠ 20°; and for D, it's (14×15°+2×40°)÷16 ≠ 20°. A) 8th B) 10th C) 12th D) 16th	30. B
31. Use 1s digits: 1+2+...+9+0 = 45. Do this 201 times, then add 1 and 2. A) 0 B) 3 C) 8 D) 9	31. C
32. The last "l" written is either the 4th or the 8th or the 12th or the ... letter written. The last "u" written is 1 less than a multiple of 4. A) 100th B) 201st C) 302nd D) 403rd	32. D
33. Every 3 steps forward is 1.5 m and every 2 backward is 1 m; so 5 steps gain 0.5 m. In 97 such sequences (485 steps), Pat has gone 48.5 m. In 3 more steps, Pat's gone 50 m. A) 100 B) 488 C) 490 D) 500	33. B
34. Gus, Hal, and Jane each try to catch the bus, and their individual probabilities of catching it are $\frac{1}{3}$, $\frac{1}{2}$, and $\frac{2}{5}$, respectively. The probability that Gus will catch the bus but Hal and Jane will not is $\frac{1}{3} \times \frac{1}{2} \times \frac{3}{5}$. A) $\frac{1}{10}$ B) $\frac{1}{15}$ C) $\frac{17}{30}$ D) $\frac{30}{17}$	34. A
35. The distance between the centers of the two circles is 5. When the small circle has gone once around the large circle, the center of the small circle will have moved 10π. Since the circumference is 2π, this circle has made 5 full rotations. A) 4 B) 5 C) 8 D) 16	35. B

The end of the contest **7**

Visit our Web site at http://www.mathleague.com

76

Information & Solutions

Tuesday, February 19 or 26, 2013

7

Contest Information

- **Solutions** Turn the page for detailed contest solutions (written in the question boxes) and letter answers (written in the *Answer Column* to the right of each question).

- **Scores** Please remember that *this is a contest, and not a test*—there is no "passing" or "failing" score. Few students score as high as 28 points (80% correct); students with half that, 14 points, *deserve commendation!*

- **Answers and Rating Scales** Turn to page 139 for the letter answers to each question and the rating scale for this contest.

1. The difference between 10.98 and 11.00 = 0.02, so 11.00 is closest.

   A) 10.00   B) 10.90   C) 10.95   D) 11.00

   1. D

2. $\sqrt{4 \times 9 \times 16} = 2 \times 3 \times 4 = 24.$

   A) 9   B) 24   C) 29   D) 36

   2. B

3. The only choice that leaves a remainder of 4 when divided into 256 is 6. Thus, Mr. Barry could have 6 cubs.

   A) 5   B) 6   C) 8   D) 11

   3. B

4. The tenths digit of 543.21 is 2, and its hundredths digit is 1.

   A) 543.21   B) 231.23   C) 654.56   D) 642.46

   4. A

5. $3^2 + 3^2 + 3^2 = 9 + 9 + 9 = 27 = 3^3.$

   A) 3^3 B) 3^6 C) 9^3 D) 9^6

   5. A

6. $3 \div \dfrac{1}{6} = (3 \times 3) \div (3 \times \dfrac{1}{6}) = 9 \div \dfrac{3}{6} = 9 \div \dfrac{1}{2}.$

   A) $\dfrac{1}{18}$ B) $\dfrac{1}{12}$ C) $\dfrac{1}{2}$ D) $\dfrac{9}{2}$

   6. C

7. Since $2013 = 3 \times 11 \times 61$ and $418 = 2 \times 11 \times 19$, the correct answer is 418.

   A) 231   B) 365   C) 418   D) 542

   7. C

8. If 3 times a number is 36, the number is 12; one-third of 12 is 4.

   A) 4   B) 12   C) 36   D) 108

   8. A

9. If a case of eggs contains $12 \times 12 = 144$ eggs, then two crates of 12 cases contain $2 \times 12 \times 144 = 3456$ eggs.

   A) 48   B) 144   C) 288   D) 3456

   9. D

10. $100\,000\,000 \div 10\,000 = 10\,000.$

    A) 10   B) 100   C) 1000   D) 10000

    10. D

11. As shown in the diagram, a diameter of the circular brim is equal to the length of a side of the square. The square has a side-length of 1 m. Since a radius of a circle is half of a diameter, the radius of the brim is 0.5 m.

    A) 0.5 m   B) 1 m   C) 2 m   D) 4 m

    11. A

12. $\dfrac{1}{\cancel{2}} \times \dfrac{\cancel{2}}{\cancel{4}} \times \dfrac{\cancel{3}}{\cancel{5}} \times \dfrac{\cancel{4}}{\cancel{6}} \times \dfrac{\cancel{5}}{7} \times \dfrac{\cancel{6}}{\cancel{8}} \times \dfrac{\cancel{7}}{9} \times \dfrac{\cancel{8}}{10} = \dfrac{1}{10} \times \dfrac{2}{9}.$

    A) $\dfrac{3}{19}$ B) $\dfrac{2}{9}$ C) $\dfrac{1}{9}$ D) $\dfrac{2}{90}$

    12. B

13. $20 + 30 + 40 - (20 + 30 + 40) \div 3 = 90 - 30 = 60.$

    A) 0   B) 45   C) 60   D) 90

    13. C

14. If 130 of Del's last meals were sandwiches, then 120 were not. Since $120 \div 250 = 0.48$, 48% of those last 250 meals were not sandwiches.

    A) 40%   B) 44%   C) 48%   D) 52%

14. C

15. The two least odd divisors of 120 are 1 and 3.

    A) 4   B) 5   C) 8   D) 15

15. A

16. Every 4×30 min. = 2 hours, I collect $4 \times 20 = 80$ seashells and drop 3 seashells. In 2 hours I have a total of 77 seashells, so in 8 hours I have $77 \times 4 = 308$ seashells.

    A) 68   B) 136   C) 296   D) 308

16. D

17. The number of nickels in $3.00 is $300 \div 5 = 60$. The number of dimes in $6.00 is $600 \div 10 = 60$. That's 120 coins; 240 quarters = $60.00.

    A) $12.00   B) $15.00   C) $30.00   D) $60.00

17. D

18. 0.05% of $10\,000 = 0.0005 \times 10\,000 = 5$.

    A) 5   B) 50   C) 500   D) 5000

18. A

19. The middle number is $13 \div 13$. The integers are $-5, -4, -3 \ldots, 5, 6$, and 7.

    A) 6   B) 7   C) 9   D) 13

19. B

20. One apple plus one orange costs $1.50. If I spend $5 \times \$1.50 = \$7.50$, I'll have $1.30 left to buy 2 more apples. That's a total of 12 pieces.

    A) 11   B) 12   C) 13   D) 14

20. B

21. Since $10 = 2 + 3 + 5$, $12 = 2 + 3 + 7$, and $15 = 3 + 5 + 7$, Dragon Doug cannot read 13 books in 3 months.

    A) 10   B) 12   C) 13   D) 15

21. C

22. The average of 45 674 567 and 67 896 789 is $(45\,674\,567 + 67\,896\,789) \div 2 = 56\,785\,678$.

    A) 55 443 322   B) 55 556 666
    C) 56 565 656   D) 56 785 678

22. D

23. $\sqrt{49} - \sqrt{16} = 7 - 4 = 3 = \sqrt{9}$.

    A) $\sqrt{33}$ B) $\sqrt{25}$ C) $\sqrt{9}$ D) $\sqrt{3}$

23. C

24. $2016^{2013} = (2^5 \times 3^2 \times 7)^{2013} = 2^{10\,065} \times 3^{4026} \times 7^{2013}$.

    A) 3^{2013} B) 3^{2015} C) 3^{4026} D) 3^{6039}

24. C

25. Friday, Mar. 4, is the 3rd day it's open. Three weeks later, Mar. 25, is the 18th day. Monday, Mar. 28, is day 19, so Mar. 30 is the 21st day.

    A) March 22   B) March 23   C) March 30   D) March 31

25. C

26. Using A, B, C, D, and E as the ingredients, the possible combinations are ABC, ABD, ABE, ACD, ACE, ADE, BCD, BCE, BDE, and CDE. A) 6 B) 8 C) 10 D) 60	26. C
27. The sum of six consecutive integers must be odd. A) 81 B) 88 C) 92 D) 98	27. A
28. 1 day = 1440 min.; 288 min. = (288/1440) = 20%. A) 10 B) 15 C) 20 D) 40	28. C
29. Two cousins visited Jane today. One cousin visits every 42 days. The other visits every 429 days. Since the l.c.m of 42 and 429 is 6006, they will next visit on the same day in 6006 days. A) 4296 B) 6006 C) 9009 D) 18018	29. B
30. $3^{2013} - 3^{2012} = 3^{2012} \times (3 - 1) = 2 \times 3^{2012}$. A) 3^1 B) 3^{2011} C) 2×3^{2012} D) 6^{1006}	30. C
31. At 3 P.M. the hands form a 90° angle; 14 mins. earlier the min. hand was $14/60 \times 360° = 84°$ back and the hr. hand was 7° back, so it's 167°. A) 84° B) 137° C) 167° D) 174°	31. C
32. The median of 6 numbers is the average of the middle ones: $(\frac{3}{4} + \frac{4}{3}) \div 2$. A) 1 B) $\frac{669}{360}$ C) $\frac{7}{12}$ D) $\frac{25}{24}$	32. D
33. This is a weighted average. Since the Master mix's sunflower percent is 10% less than the Blue mix's and 15% more than the Rye mix's, the ratio of Blue mix to Rye mix is 15:10. (The ratio is the reverse of the percents.) Thus, 15/25 of the Master mix is Blue mix. In 1000 g the part that is Blue mix is $15/25 \times 1000 = 600$ g. A) 350 g B) 400 g C) 600 g D) 650 g	33. C
34. There are 50 multiples of 2 on the list, 25 multiples of 4, 12 of 8, 6 of 16, 3 of 32, and 1 of 64. That's 2^{97} or 2×4^{48}. A) 4^{25} B) 4^{32} C) 4^{48} D) 4^{50}	34. C
35. The ratio of the fraction of new books that are biographies to the fraction of used books that are biographies is (0.7/0.85) : (0.3/0.15). This is equivalent to (7/85) : (3/15) = (7/85) : (17/85). This simplifies to 7 : 17. A) 7:17 B) 14:17 C) 17:14 D) 17:7	35. A

The end of the contest ✍ **7**

Visit our Web site at http://www.mathleague.com

Information & Solutions

Tuesday, February 18 or 25, 2014

7

Contest Information

- **Solutions** Turn the page for detailed contest solutions (written in the question boxes) and letter answers (written in the *Answer Column* to the right of each question).

- **Scores** Please remember that *this is a contest, and not a test* — there is no "passing" or "failing" score. Few students score as high as 28 points (80% correct); students with half that, 14 points, *deserve commendation!*

- **Answers and Rating Scales** Turn to page 140 for the letter answers to each question and the rating scale for this contest.

1. $2014 \times 4 - 2014 \times 2 = 2014 \times (4 - 2) = 2014 \times 2$.

   A) −   B) +   C) ×   D) ÷

   1.
   A

2. Mr. Spud inspects 20 potatoes per hour, 8 hours per day. In 5 days he inspects a total of $20 \times 8 \times 5 = 800$ potatoes.

   A) 33   B) 160   C) 165   D) 800

   2.
   D

3. $(2 \times 12 \times 5) \div (2 \times 5) = 12$.

   A) 6   B) 8   C) 10   D) 12

   3.
   C

4. I am 20th in line and my friend is 10th in line. The people between us are 11th, 12th, 13th, . . . , and 19th in line. That's 9 people.

   A) 8   B) 9   C) 10   D) 11

   4.
   B

5. There are 24 socks in a drawer, and half are black socks. There are 12 black socks = $12 \div 2 = 6$ pairs of black socks in the drawer.

   A) 4   B) 6   C) 12   D) 24

   5.
   B

6. A pentagon has 5 sides.

   A) rhombus   B) trapezoid   C) pentagon   D) hexagon

   6.
   C

7. $5 + 25 + 125 = 5 \times (1 + 5 + 25) = 5 \times 31$.

   A) 6   B) 15   C) 25   D) 31

   7.
   D

8. The integers from 55 to 66 with a ones digit greater than the tens digit are 56, 57, 58, and 59. That's a total of 4 numbers.

   A) 4   B) 5   C) 10   D) 11

   8.
   A

9. The sum of the digits of 371 is 2 more than a multiple of 3.

   A) 371   B) 456   C) 523   D) 676

   9.
   A

10. Since the change Lex receives is twice the price of a book, the cost of 8 books is $50 and the cost of one book is $50÷8 = $6.25.

    A) $6.25   B) $7.14   C) $8.33   D) $12.50

    10.
    A

11. Sam skateboarded until 6:16 PM. Sam skateboarded for 66 minutes. First count backwards 60 minutes to 5:16 PM, then count back 6 more minutes to 5:10 PM.

    A) 5:00 P.M.   B) 5:10 P.M.
    C) 5:22 P.M.   D) 5:30 P.M.

    11.
    B

12. $7 < 222 \div 31 < 222 \div 30 < 8$; it's the 8th month.

    A) May   B) June   C) July   D) August

    12.
    D

13. Each side of the equilateral triangle has length $18 \div 3 = 6$. The perimeter of a square with sides of length 6 is $4 \times 6 = 24$.

    A) 18   B) 24   C) 36   D) 90

    13.
    B

Go on to the next page)))▶ **7**

14. The number of heart balloons that Cora has is
divisible by three different primes. Cora must
have at least 2 × 3 × 5 = 30 balloons.

A) 6   B) 10   C) 15   D) 30

15. Since 10 000 ÷ 13 = 769 R3, the greatest multiple of
13 less than 10 000 is 9997. Its ones digit is 7.

A) 3   B) 6   C) 7   D) 9

16. (10×25¢) + (30×10¢) = (50×5¢) + (60×5¢) = 110×5¢.

A) 50   B) 60   C) 100   D) 110

17. If 2 quonks = 6 quinks, 1 quonk = 3 quinks. Hence
1 quonk = 8 quanks and 8 quonks = 64 quanks.

A) 8   B) 16   C) 24   D) 32

18. The average of any number of sixes is always 6.

A) threes   B) sixes   C) nines   D) twelves

19. The factors of 120 that are divisible by 3 are 3, 6, 12, 15, 24, 30, 60, 120.

A) 7   B) 8   C) 9   D) 10

20. 0.625% of 8% of 500 = (5/8)% × 8% × 500 = (5/8)% × 40 = 0.25.

A) 0.25   B) 2.5   C) 25   D) 250

21. Dr. Craven sees that for every 2 people in the audience
who are smiling, there are 7 who are not. The
number of people in the audience must be a
multiple of 2 + 7 = 9.

A) 77   B) 85   C) 99   D) 105

22. Since 3 + 5 is not greater than 9, the third side
cannot have length 3.

A) 3   B) 6   C) 9   D) 12

23. The sum of the greatest 3-digit prime and the
least 3-digit prime is 997 + 101 = 1098.

A) 1094   B) 1096   C) 1098   D) 1100

24. Since the number of pencils in my backpack is 4 more than a multiple
of 6, twice the number is 8 more than a multiple of 6. The extra 8
gives another 6, with remainder 2.

A) 0   B) 2   C) 4   D) 8

25. Since the sum is 23 kg, the weights (in kg) could be 1 & 22, 2 & 21, . . . , or
11 & 12. The correct pair is 9 & 14, so the heavier fish weighs 14 kg.

A) 9 kg   B) 12 kg   C) 14 kg   D) 19 kg

Go on to the next page))))➡ **7**

26. If $\frac{1}{5}$ of the 200 stripes on the shell are blue, 160 are not blue. Thus $\frac{2}{5}$ (64) of these 160 stripes are brown; the rest, 96, are white. There are 56 more white stripes than blue stripes.

    A) 0   B) 40   C) 42   D) 56

26.

D

27. If 5/4 of a number is 160, 1/4 is 32 and 3/4 is 96.

    A) 82   B) 88   C) 90   D) 96

27.

D

28. Starting at 1, subtract squares from 17^2 until the difference is a square: $17^2 - 8^2 = 15^2$, so sum is 23.

    A) 23   B) 25   C) 27   D) 29

28.

A

29. $\frac{1}{13} = 0.\overline{076923}$; the 4th, 10th, 16th, . . . , 94th, and 100th digits are 9s.

    A) 9   B) 6   C) 3   D) 2

29.

A

30. The sum of Bei's & Fay's ages is 24. The sum of Ray's & Clyde's ages is 32. The sum of Bei's, Fay's, & Ray's ages is 33. Clyde is $24 + 32 - 33$.

    A) 28   B) 23   C) 20   D) 17

30.

B

31. Use R, B, G, O, Y, and W for the colors. With either R or B, Kim can have G-O, G-Y, G-W, O-Y, O-W, or Y-W. Without R or B, she can have G-O-Y, G-O-W, G-Y-W, or O-Y-W. That's a total of 16 combos.

    A) 16   B) 32   C) 64   D) 120

31.

A

32. $\frac{5^{95} - 5^{94}}{2^2} = \frac{5^{94} \times (5-1)}{2^2} = 5^{94}$.

    A) 1.25   B) $5^{91} - 5^{90}$ C) $5^{93} - 5^{92}$ D) 5^{94}

32.

D

33. Try 200. If 200 girls won for math, comprising 2/3 of the math winners, then 100 boys won for math. That leaves 200 certificates for science, 100 for boys and 100 for girls. Is 200 actually 50 more than 3/2 of 100? Yes, so 200 is the answer.

    A) 200   B) 275   C) 300   D) 350

33.

A

34. Choose the midpoint of each side as a vertex to get the minimum area of 200.

    A) 100   B) 160   C) 200   D) 250

34.

C

35. The numbers in the sequence have remainders of 0, 3, or 4 when divided by 9. Since 733 divided by 9 has remainder 4, it is included.

    A) 694   B) 733   C) 812   D) 950

35.

B

The end of the contest ✍ **7**

Visit our Web site at http://www.mathleague.com

Information & Solutions

Tuesday, February 17 or 24, 2015

7

Contest Information

- **Solutions** Turn the page for detailed contest solutions (written in the question boxes) and letter answers (written in the *Answer Column* to the right of each question).

- **Scores** Please remember that *this is a contest, and not a test*—there is no "passing" or "failing" score. Few students score as high as 28 points (80% correct); students with half that, 14 points, *deserve commendation!*

- **Answers and Rating Scales** Turn to page 141 for the letter answers to each question and the rating scale for this contest.

1. $2 \times 0 + 1 \times 4 - 2 \times 0 + 1 \times 5 = 0 + 4 - 0 + 5 = 9.$

    A) 0   B) 5   C) 9   D) 15

2. There are 84 beavers in a colony. There were $84 \div 6 = 14$ teams of 6. There are $84 \div 4 = 21$ teams of 4. There will be 7 more teams today than there were yesterday.

    A) 2   B) 7   C) 14   D) 21

3. $12345 + 54321 = 66666 = 11111 \times 6.$

    A) 66666   B) 666   C) 66   D) 6

4. Since 192 months = $(192 \div 12)$ years, my brother is 16 years old. I am $(16 \div 2)$ years old = 8 years old.

    A) 8   B) 16   C) 32   D) 96

5. Apples cost $1.25 each, or 3 for $3. If I want to buy 11 apples, I can buy 9 apples for $9 and 2 apples for $2.50. That's a total of $11.50.

    A) $11.00   B) $11.50   C) $12.00   D) $13.75

6. Multiplying by $\frac{2}{3}$ is the same as dividing by its reciprocal, $\frac{3}{2}$.

    A) 0.667   B) 0.75   C) 1.5   D) 1.667

7. Since multiples of 4 are divisible by 4, none are prime.

    A) 0   B) 6   C) 7   D) 8

8. If my average for 4 tests is 86, the sum of the 4 scores is $4 \times 86 = 344$. Since $80 + 84 + 94 = 258$, I must score $344 - 258 = 86$ on the next test.

    A) 0   B) 86   C) 87   D) 88

9. The sum of the lengths of 2 sides of a triangle > the length of the 3rd side. Since $2 + 4$ is **not** > 6, 6 cannot be the length of the longest side.

    A) 6   B) 10   C) 12   D) 16

10. An increase from 8 to 10 is an increase of 2/8 = 25%.

    A) 2%   B) 10%   C) 20%   D) 25%

11. $(25 \times 3)^2 \times 25 = 25^2 \times 3^2 \times 5^2 = 25^2 \times (3 \times 5)^2.$

    A) 3^2 B) 5^2 C) 75   D) 15^2

12. If 123 were the sum of 2 primes, one must be 2.

    A) $2+3$ B) $3+5$ C) $2+121$ D) $2+7$

13. The product of a circle's circumference and radius divided by its area is $2\pi r \times r \div \pi r^2 = 2.$

    A) 2   B) π C) 2π D) $2\pi^2$

Answers
1. C
2. B
3. D
4. A
5. B
6. C
7. A
8. B
9. A
10. D
11. D
12. C
13. A

14. In 1 day Mr. Wells will be 80% visible. In 2 days, he will be 80% of 80% visible or 64% visible. In 3 days, he will be 80% of 64% visible or 51.2% visible. In 4 days he will be 80% of 51.2% visible or 40.96% visible.

A) 3   B) 4   C) 5   D) 6

14.

B

15. $1\frac{1}{3} \times 1\frac{1}{4} \times 1\frac{1}{5} = \frac{4}{3} \times \frac{5}{4} \times \frac{6}{5} = \frac{6}{3} = 2.$

A) 2   B) 3   C) $1\frac{1}{6}$ D) $1\frac{1}{60}$

15.

A

16. $1\,000\,000\,000 = 10^9$; its only prime factors are 2 and 5.

A) 1   B) 2   C) 5   D) 10

16.

C

17. $999\,999 \times (999\,999 - 1) = (999\,999 \times 999\,999) - 999\,999.$

A) 1   B) 999\,997   C) 999\,998   D) 999\,999

17.

D

18. Ten years from two years ago, I will be twice my age two years ago; I will be 20 years old then. I am 12 now and will be 14 in 2 years.

A) 14   B) 16   C) 18   D) 20

18.

A

19. If I try 5 nickels and 5 pennies, I have 30¢. The combined value of my quarters and nickels is 300¢. The 5 nickels are worth 25¢, leaving 275¢ or 11 quarters. (Try any multiple of 5 for the # of nickels.)

A) 1:1   B) 2:1   C) 10:3   D) 11:5

19.

D

20. Change 0.75 to a fraction and find equivalent fractions: 0.75 = 3/4 = 6/8 = 9/12 = . . . = 72/96. Since 96 = 4×24, there are 24 such fractions.

A) 3   B) 24   C) 25   D) 33

20.

B

21. The Skippers' average rowing rate is the same as their rate during the 3rd hour. If their rate for the 3rd hour is 6 km/hr, then they rowed 6 km during the 3rd hour, 8 km during the 2nd hour, and 10 km during the 1st hour. That's (8 + 10) km in the first 2 hours.

A) 6   B) 12   C) 16   D) 18

21.

D

22. $500 - 200 = 300; 300 = 150\%$ of 200.

A) 50   B) 150   C) 250   D) 300

22.

B

23. $9^2 < 100 < 11^2 < 31^2 < 1000 < 33^2$; the squares of 11, 13, . . . , 31 work.

A) 11   B) 16   C) 21   D) 31

23.

A

24. The side-length is 90; the area is 8100. Thus, $8100 \div 9 = 900$ squares.

A) 40   B) 400   C) 900   D) 1600

24. C

25. The largest odd factor of $(3\times2)^6 \times (5\times2)^{10}$ is $3^6 \times 5^{10}$.

A) $6^5 \times 10^9$ B) $6^3 \times 10^5$ C) $3^6 \times 5^{10}$ D) $3^3 \times 5^5$

25.

C

26. Greg paid Ori $4 × 150 for typing each page once. Then Greg paid Ori $2 × 30 for retyping 30 pages. Finally Greg paid Ori $2 × 15 for typing 15 pages another time. In all, Greg paid Ori $600 + $60 + $30 = $690.

    A) $660   B) $690   C) $720   D) $760

26.

B

27. Of the 9 factors of 10^2, 4 are factors of 10.

    A) $\dfrac{1}{10}$ B) $\dfrac{4}{9}$ C) $\dfrac{5}{9}$ D) $\dfrac{9}{10}$

27.

B

28. Choice B is divisible by 3, and choices C and D are both even.

    A) $29^2 + 66^2$ B) $42^2 + 45^2$ C) $22^2 + 64^2$ D) $32^2 + 54^2$

28.

A

29. Since 1890 ÷ 360 = 5R90, this rotation is the same as a 90° rotation. Therefore, B will be at the top.

    A) A   B) B   C) C   D) D

29.

B

30. The lcm of 2^2, 2^4, $2^2 × 3^2$, 2^6, and $2^2 × 5^2$ is $2^6 × 3^2 × 5^2 = 14\,400$.

    A) 3840   B) 14 400   C) 57 600   D) 230 400

30.

B

31. A snail crawls 2400 mm/3600 sec = 2 mm/3 sec = 1 mm/1.5 sec.

    A) $\dfrac{1}{3}$ B) $\dfrac{2}{3}$ C) 1.5   D) 3

31.

C

32. A circle can intersect each side 2, 1, or 0 times. Find all possible sums.

    A) 0, 2 or 8 only   B) 0, 2, 4, 6 or 8 only
    C) 1, 2, 3, 4, 6, or 8 only   D) 0, 1, 2, 3, 4, 5, 6, 7, or 8

32.

D

33. There are 26 1-letter codes, 26^2 2-letter codes, and 26^3 3-letter codes. That's a total of 26 + 676 + 17 576 = 18 278 different codes, so Carla has 18 278 shells.

    A) 156   B) 17 576   C) 18 278   D) 20 888

33.

C

34. Each of the next 50 integers is 50 > the corresponding earlier one. Their sum is 50×50 more than 1525.

    A) 1575   B) 2775   C) 4025   D) 76 250

34.

C

35. There are 4 ways to choose 3 pairs of twins and 2 ways to choose one person from each pair. That's a total of 4 × 2 × 2 × 2 = 32 different groups.

    A) 16   B) 24   C) 28   D) 32

35.

D

The end of the contest ☜ **7**

Visit our Web site at http://www.mathleague.com

Information & Solutions

Tuesday, February 16 or 23, 2016

7

Contest Information

- **Solutions** Turn the page for detailed contest solutions (written in the question boxes) and letter answers (written in the *Answer Column* to the right of each question).

- **Scores** Please remember that *this is a contest, and not a test*—there is no "passing" or "failing" score. Few students score as high as 28 points (80% correct); students with half that, 14 points, *deserve commendation!*

- **Answers and Rating Scales** Turn to page 142 for the letter answers to each question and the rating scale for this contest.

1. $(2+0+1+6) \times (6+1+0+2) = 9 \times 9 = 3^2 \times 3^2 = 3^4$. A) 3^2 B) 3^3 C) 3^4 D) 3^6	1. C
2. Of the 77 7th graders in my school, $\frac{3}{7}$ are boys. That's 33 boys and 44 girls. A) 30 B) 33 C) 40 D) 44	2. D
3. $2016\,000\,000 = 2.016 \times 1\,000\,000\,000$ A) 10^6 B) 10^7 C) 10^8 D) 10^9	3. D
4. If English took 9000 seconds, math took 4500 seconds = $4500 \div 60$ minutes = 75 minutes. A) 15 B) 45 C) 75 D) 150	4. C
5. (A number) + (-5) = (a number) -5. A) 5 B) -5 C) 1/5 D) -1/5	5. A
6. The reciprocal of 0.4 is 5/2. A) 0.2 B) 0.4 C) 0.5 D) 1	6. B
7. $80 \times 36 + 80 \times 14 = 80 \times (36 + 14) = 80 \times 50$. A) 50 B) 60 C) 130 D) 504	7. A
8. The square root of 2016 is between 44 and 45, so choice B is correct. A) 43 B) 44 C) 45 D) 46	8. B
9. The greatest prime number less than 100 that can itself be expressed as the sum of two prime numbers is 73 since $73 = 2 + 71$. A) 91 B) 89 C) 79 D) 73	9. D
10. The l.c.m. of each in order are 56, 44, 48, and 36. Choice A is greatest. A) 7 and 8 B) 4 and 11 C) 12 and 16 D) 6 and 36	10. A
11. If I travel at 6 m/sec, I will get home in 4 minutes. My trip is 6×240 = 1440 m. If I travel at 8 m/sec, the trip will take me $1440 \div 8 = 180$ seconds = 3 minutes, 1 minute fewer. A) 1 B) 3 C) 4 D) 60	11. A
12. 49 is a perfect square. The product of two perfect squares is a perfect square. A) prime B) odd C) even D) a perfect square	12. D
13. $3 \times 9 \times 27 = 3^1 \times 3^2 \times 3^3 = 3^{1+2+3} = 3^6$. A) 3^3 B) 3^4 C) 3^5 D) 3^6	13. D

Go on to the next page)))► 7

14. The first number said will be 10 000, then
$\sqrt{10000} = 100$, then $\sqrt{100} = 10$. Since $\sqrt{10}$
is between 3 and 4, the next number said
will be 3. Next, $\sqrt{3}$ is between 1 and 2,
so the next and final number said will
be 1. Squaroo says "10 000, 100, 10, 3, 1," a
total of 5 numbers.

A) 4   B) 5   C) 6   D) 7

14.

B

15. The only common factor of two integers that differ by 1 is 1.

A) 1   B) 2   C) 3   D) 4

15.

A

16. 2015 is divisible by 5. Both 2016 and 2018 are divisible by 2.

A) 2015   B) 2016   C) 2017   D) 2018

16.

C

17. 1864 is not divisible by 3, 6, or 9. Only Choice C is correct.

A) 3   B) 6   C) 8   D) 9

17.

C

18. For every 5 boys, there are 2 more girls than boys. There are 10
more girls than boys, so there are 5 × 5 boys and 5 × 7 girls.

A) 25   B) 30   C) 35   D) 40

18.

A

19. The area of A is 16. The area of B is 144. The side-length of B is 12, so
the perimeter of B is 48.

A) 12   B) 36   C) 48   D) 144

19.

C

20. Let p be a prime. The positive integer factors of
p^5 are 1, p, p^2, p^3, p^4, and p^5. There are 6 of them.

A) 5   B) 6   C) 32   D) 120

20.

B

21. $111 \times 89 = (100 + 11)(100 - 11) = 100^2 - 121$.

A) 10   B) 11   C) 100   D) 121

21.

D

22. There are 250 even numbers from 1 to 500. Half
of these are not divisible by 4.

A) 122   B) 123   C) 124   D) 125

22.

D

23. $95 = 19 \times 5$; $119 = 17 \times 7$; $143 = 13 \times 11$.
($63 = 3 \times 3 \times 7$, which is more than 2 primes.)

A) 63   B) 95   C) 119   D) 143

23.

A

24. Increasing the side-length from 10 to 15 increases the area by 125.

A) 25%   B) 50%   C) 125%   D) 225%

24.

C

25. Only 115, 151, and 511 consist of exactly 3 digits with a product of 5.

A) 4   B) 3   C) 2   D) 1

25.

B

Go on to the next page ⟫➡ **7**

26. The product of the hundreds and ones digits must be a perfect square. The numbers with that property and a hundreds digit of 1 have a ones digit of 0, 1, 4, or 9. The possibilities with the appropriate middle digit are 100, 111, 124, and 139. Only 139 can be reached by adding; 139 − 124 = 15 gumballs are added.

   A) 209   B) 124   C) 98   D) 15

26.

D

27. 1+(1+2+4+8+16+32+64+128+256) = 1+511 = 512 = 2^9.

   A) 2^8 B) 2^9 C) 2^{10} D) 2^{11}

27.

B

28. Since 30 students study both math and English, there are 60 − 30 = 30 students who study only math and 70 − 30 = 40 students who study only English. There are 30 + 30 + 40 = 100 students.

   A) 100   B) 130   C) 160   D) 190

28.

A

29. The sum of the lengths of 2 sides > the length of the 3rd side; 35 − 20 = 15 and 35 + 20 = 55; the 3rd side's length ranges from 16 to 54.

   A) 37   B) 38   C) 39   D) 40

29.

C

30. The numbers for choices B, C, and D are divisible by 3, 11, and 11 111.

   A) 19   B) 21   C) 22   D) 25

30.

A

31. The ones digit of 2016^{2016} is 6; 2017^{2017} has the same ones digit as 2017^1.

   A) 3   B) 5   C) 7   D) 9

31.

A

32. If 3 people have birthdays in each month, the number of people at the party is 36. If 1 more person attends, 4 people must have birthdays in the same month.

   A) 15   B) 16   C) 36   D) 37

32.

D

33. $9^{1010} − 3^{2016} = 3^{2020} − 3^{2016} = 3^{2016} \times 80$.

   A) 3   B) 5   C) 7   D) 13

33.

B

34. There are 5^4 such integers whose average is 5555. Multiply 5555 by 5^4.

   A) 138 875   B) 694 375   C) 3 471 875   D) 17 359 375

34.

C

35. Two different circles can intersect in at most 2 points. The third circle can add 4 intersection points, and so on. We have 2 + 4 + 6 + 8 + 10 + 12 = 42.

   A) 20   B) 30   C) 35   D) 42

35.

D

The end of the contest 7

Visit our Web site at http://www.mathleague.com

8th Grade Solutions

2011-2012 through 2015-2016

Information & Solutions

Tuesday, February 21 or 28, 2012

8

Contest Information

- **Solutions** Turn the page for detailed contest solutions (written in the question boxes) and letter answers (written in the *Answer Column* to the right of each question).

- **Scores** Please remember that *this is a contest, and not a test*—there is no "passing" or "failing" score. Few students score as high as 28 points (80% correct); students with half that, 14 points, *deserve commendation!*

- **Answers and Rating Scales** Turn to page 143 for the letter answers to each question and the rating scale for this contest.

1. Explorer Rick sees 2012 animals. Half are 2-legged and half are 4-legged. Rick sees $2 \times 1006 + 4 \times 1006 = 6036$ legs.

   A) 4024   B) 6036   C) 8048   D) 12072

   1.
   B

2. Order of operations: $(1000 \div 100) + (10 \times 0) = 10$.

   A) 0   B) 10   C) 100   D) 1000

   2.
   B

3. The largest tenths digit is in 0.321.

   A) 0.123   B) 0.321   C) 0.0123   D) 0.0321

   3.
   B

4. The 8 primes are 2, 3, 5, 7, 11, 13, 17, and 19; $8 \div 20 = 0.4 = 40\%$. (Note: 1 is not a prime.)

   A) 8%   B) 9%   C) 40%   D) 45%

   4.
   C

5. Since the oldest brother is twice as old as the youngest, their ages could be 2 and 1, 4 and 2, 6 and 3, 8 and 4, 10 and 5, ... Only ages 8 and 4 allow for the ages to be 5 consecutive numbers: 4, 5, 6, 7, 8.

   A) 3   B) 4   C) 5   D) 6

   5.
   D

6. To get the ones digit of the product, multiply the ones digit of each of the product's 10 factors: $1 \times 2 \times 3 \times 4 \times 5 \times 6 \times 7 \times 8 \times 9 \times 0 = 0$.

   A) 0   B) 1   C) 5   D) 9

   6.
   A

7. The triangle cannot be a right triangle since the hypotenuse of a right triangle is longer than either of the other two sides.

   A) isosceles   B) equilateral   C) acute   D) right

   7.
   D

8. 20% of $50 = 0.2 \times 50 = (0.2 \times 10) \times (50 \div 10) = 2 \times 5 = 200\%$ of 5.

   A) 2% of 0.5   B) 5% of 0.2   C) 200% of 5   D) 500% of 20

   8.
   C

9. Sheriff Sam's slingshot slings 0.7 g of berries. If the slingshot slings 70 kg of berries, it slings $(70000 \text{ g} \div 0.7 \text{ g}) = 100000$ berries.

   A) 1000   B) 10000   C) 100000   D) 1000000

   9.
   C

10. There are 6 days between any two consecutive Sundays, so the number of days is $(29 \times 6) + 30 = 204$.

    A) 210   B) 204   C) 198   D) 192

    10.
    B

11. If $\frac{2}{3}$ of a certain number is 200, then the certain number is 300; $\frac{3}{2}$ of 300 is 450.

    A) 200   B) 400   C) 450   D) 600

    11.
    C

12. $(100 + -100) + (200 + -200) + 300 = 300$; the average is $300 \div 5 = 60$.

    A) 60   B) 150   C) 200   D) 300

    12.
    A

Go on to the next page ⟫⟫ **8**

13. I dropped a rock every 8 m, a coin every 12 m, and a frog every 18 m. Since the least common multiple of 8, 12, and 18 is 72, I first dropped all three items when I had walked 72 m. A) 38 m B) 72 m C) 128 m D) 1728 m	13. B
14. Since $\frac{2}{3} + \frac{4}{5} = \frac{10}{15} + \frac{12}{15} = \frac{22}{15} \times \frac{3}{3} = \frac{66}{45}$, it's C. A) 15 B) 30 C) 45 D) 88	14. C
15. He walks 5 km/hr. = 40 km/8 hr. = 40 km/day. Each week he walks 6 days × 40 km/day = 240 km. It takes him 3600 km ÷ 240 km/week = 15 weeks. A) 15 B) 20 C) 30 D) 60	15. A
16. A cube has 6 faces and 12 edges, and 6 + 12 = 18. A) 12 B) 14 C) 16 D) 18	16. D
17. My lemonade recipe requires $\frac{3}{2}$ ℓ of water to make 24 servings. I want 30 servings. Since 30:24 = 5:4, I need $\frac{5}{4} \times \frac{3}{2}$ ℓ $= \frac{15}{8}$ ℓ of water. A) $\frac{7}{8}$ ℓ B) $\frac{15}{8}$ ℓ C) $\frac{7}{4}$ ℓ D) $\frac{15}{4}$ ℓ	17. B
18. The average value of 30 nickels and 10 quarters is (150¢ + 250¢) ÷ 40 = 10¢. A) 10¢ B) 15¢ C) 20¢ D) 30¢	18. A
19. Calculate the difference between each choice and its reciprocal; 1.001 – 1/1.001 has the smallest difference. (Note that 1.001 is closest to 1.) A) 1.001 B) 1.01 C) 1.111 D) 1.2	19. A
20. Since 11 have neither, 56 – 11 = 45 have blue eyes and/or spots; so 34 have spots, 45–34 = 11 spotless dogs have blue eyes, and 23–11 have both. A) 6 B) 12 C) 24 D) 31	20. B
21. Since 40 kg is 80% of his original weight, his original weight = 40 kg ÷ 0.80 = 50 kg. A) 42 B) 44 C) 48 D) 50	21. D
22. The product of 3 integers is 60. Their sum *cannot* be A) 3+4+5 B) 2+3+10 C) 1+5+12 D) 22	22. D
23. A and C are odd if *n* = 2; B is odd if *n* = 1. A) *n* + 1 B) *n* + 2 C) 2×*n*+1 D) 2×*n*+2	23. D
24. $(200^3 \times 200^3)^6 \div 200^9 = (200^6)^6 \div 200^9 = 200^{36} \div 200^9 = 200^{27}$. A) 200^4 B) 200^6 C) 200^{27} D) 200^{45}	24. C
25. Multiply pairs of factors to find the number: 5×65 = 13×25 = 325 = 1×itself. A) 325 B) 845 C) 1625 D) 105 625	25. A

26. Since 56 is seven-eighths of 64, Darius has 64 paintings in all. His total cost was $(8 \times 60) + (56 \times 90) = 5520$ bones.

A) 5340   B) 5400   C) 5460   D) 5520

26.

D

27. A circle of area 64π has $r = 8$ and circumference 16π. The 2nd circle's circumference is $100\pi - 16\pi = 84\pi$. Its radius is 42, so its area is $42^2 \times \pi = 1764\pi$.

A) 36π B) 56π C) 136π D) 1764π

27.

D

28. For each of the choices, the order of the points P, Q, R, and S is shown next to the answer choice. Of the choices listed, only 9 cannot be the distance from P to S.

A) 3 (*P,S,Q,R*)   B) 5 (*R,P,Q,S*)   C) 7 (*S,R,P,Q*)   D) 9

28.

D

29. $21^{21} + 21^{22} = 21^{21} \times (1 + 21) = 21^{21} \times 22$.

A) 21^{43} B) $21^{21} \times 22$ C) $2 \times 21^{21} + 21$ D) $2 \times 21^{22} - 21$

29.

B

30. If the sum of the digits of 12, 24, 36, or 48 is multiplied by 4, the product is the original integer. There are only 4 such 2-digit integers.

A) 1   B) 2   C) 4   D) 8

30.

C

31. Since $m\angle 1 + m\angle 2 = 180 = m\angle C + m\angle 3 + m\angle 2$, $m\angle 1 = m\angle C + m\angle 3$. But $m\angle 1 = 2 \times m\angle C$. Thus, $m\angle 3 = m\angle C$ and $BC = BD = 8$. Since $m\angle A = m\angle 1$, $BD = AD = 8$.

A) 4   B) 8   C) 12   D) 16

31.

B

32. Use the Pythagorean Theorem. Since $360^2 + 780^2 \neq 850^2$, C is correct.

A) 238 m north, then 816 m east   B) 510 m north, then 680 m east
C) 360 m north, then 780 m east   D) 400 m north, then 750 m east

32.

C

33. There are three possible choices for each digit, so there are $3 \times 3 \times 3 = 27$ such three-digit numbers in all.

A) 6   B) 9   C) 18   D) 27

33.

D

34. Try to find integer ratios equivalent to 2:5 with a difference equal to each choice. Since 2:5 = 160:400 and $400 - 160 = 240$, A works. Now check: Subtract 20 from numerator, add 20 to denom.; ratio is 1:3.

A) 240 cm   B) 260 cm   C) 280 cm   D) 320 cm

34.

A

35. Let the 3 numbers be AB, AC, and DB. There are 9 possible choices for A and 8 possible choices for D since neither can be 0. Similarly, there are 10 choices for B and then 9 choices for C. In all there are $9 \times 8 \times 10 \times 9 = 6480$ possibilities.

A) 6480   B) 7200   C) 7290   D) 8100

35.

A

The end of the contest **8**

Visit our Web site at http://www.mathleague.com

Information & Solutions

Tuesday, February 19 or 26, 2013

8

Contest Information

- **Solutions** Turn the page for detailed contest solutions (written in the question boxes) and letter answers (written in the *Answer Column* to the right of each question).

- **Scores** Please remember that *this is a contest, and not a test*—there is no "passing" or "failing" score. Few students score as high as 28 points (80% correct); students with half that, 14 points, *deserve commendation!*

- **Answers and Rating Scales** Turn to page 144 for the letter answers to each question and the rating scale for this contest.

1. Since $1 + 4 + 1 + 4 = 10$, $(1 + 4 + 1 + 4) \times 1414 = 14\,140$.

   A) 10   B) 1010   C) 1414   D) 10000

   1.

   C

2. Any number divisible by 2 and 5 ends in 0. Only 6660 ends in 0 and is also divisible by 3 and 4.

   A) 2345   B) 4567
   C) 5550   D) 6660

   2.

   D

3. $(25 + 4001) \div 2 = 2013$.

   A) 994   B) 1019   C) 1988   D) 4001

   3.

   D

4. Bob rides his bicycle at 40 km per 60 minutes. In 30 minutes he rides 20 km, so in 3 minutes he rides 2 km.

   A) 1 km   B) 2 km   C) 3 km   D) 4 km

   4.

   B

5. There are 9 people in front of my brother, and there are 9 people behind me. That's 18 people. Counting my brother and me, that's a total of 20 people in line.

   A) 11   B) 19   C) 20   D) 21

   5.

   C

6. Of every 5 books, 4 have hard covers. Since $60 \div 5 = 12$, there are 12 groups of 5 books each. Since $12 \times 4 = 48$, I have 48 hard covers.

   A) 48   B) 35   C) 15   D) 12

   6.

   A

7. Since $111 = 1 \times 111$, the largest odd factor of 111 is 111.

   A) 3   B) 37   C) 109   D) 111

   7.

   D

8. 100 pennies = \$1; 200 nickels = $200 \times 5¢ = \$10$; 300 dimes = $300 \times 10¢ = \$30$; and 400 quarters = $400 \times 25¢ = \$100$; the coins' value is \$141.

   A) \$91   B) \$121   C) \$141   D) \$161

   8.

   C

9. Multiply the last 3 digits of each: 789×890 = 702 210; the hundreds digit is 2.

   A) 0   B) 1   C) 2   D) 3

   9.

   C

10. Ben finds 2 eyes under 40% of the rocks. If he looks under 400 rocks, he will find $2 \times 0.4 \times 400 = 320$ eyes.

    A) 100   B) 160   C) 200   D) 320

    10.

    D

11. $\cancel{12} \times \dfrac{1}{\cancel{2}} \times \dfrac{1}{3} \times \dfrac{1}{4} \times \dfrac{1}{\cancel{6}} =$

    A) $\dfrac{1}{144}$ B) $\dfrac{1}{12}$ C) 1   D) 12

    11.

    B

12. If the measures of the angles of triangle T are in a 1:2:3 ratio, they must have measures 30°, 60°, and 90°. So T is a right triangle.

    A) acute   B) obtuse   C) right   D) isosceles

    12.

    C

Go on to the next page))))➤ **8**

13. $(9+8) \times 6 - 4 \div 2 = 17 \times 6 - 2 = 100$.

   A) $9+8 \times 6 - 4 \div 2$ B) $(9+8) \times 6 - 4 \div 2$
   C) $9+8 \times (6-4) \div 2$ D) $(9+8) \times (6-4) \div 2$

13.
B

14. The least common multiple of $2 \times 3 \times 3$, $2 \times 2 \times 7$, and 2×19 is $2 \times 2 \times 3 \times 3 \times 7 \times 19 = 4788$. Thus, Alex found 4788 diamonds.

   A) 2   B) 84   C) 4788   D) 19 152

14.
C

15. $0.07 + 0.007 = 0.077 = 0.700 - 0.623$.

   A) 0.623   B) 0.777   C) 0.784   D) 0.854

15.
A

16. $2^2 \times 2^2 \times 2^2 + 2^2 \times 2^2 + 2^2 = 4 \times 4 \times 4 + 4 \times 4 + 4 = 64 + 16 + 4 = 84 = 2^2 \times 21$.

   A) 16   B) 21   C) 32   D) 33

16.
B

17. Multiplying any whole number by 6 results in a product divisible by 3; after adding 5, the sum can no longer be divisible by 3 or 9.

   A) 5   B) 7   C) 9   D) 11

17.
C

18. Divide 10000 hours by 24 hours per day to find that it is 416 days, 16 hours. The princess wakes 16 hours after 6:00 P.M., at 10:00 A.M.

   A) 10:00 A.M.   B) 4:00 P.M.   C) 8:00 P.M.   D) 11:00 P.M.

18.
A

19. Since $40\% + 1/3 = 2/5 + 1/3 = 11/15$, the remaining $4/15$ are the 60 metamorphic rocks. Hence $4:15 = 60:?$, and $? = 225$.

   A) 160   B) 180   C) 200   D) 225

19.
D

20. The sum of 4 consecutive even integers is 148. Their average is 37. The 4 integers are 34, 36, 38, and 40. The sum of the digits of 34 is 7.

   A) 6   B) 7   C) 9   D) 12

20.
B

21. Since $108 \div 9 = 12$, Max has $12 \times 2 = 24$ surfboards.

   A) 12   B) 24   C) 48   D) 486

21.
B

22. $180 + 180 \times 1.5 = 180 + 270 = 450$.

   A) 270   B) 330   C) 450   D) 630

22.
C

23. The longest side's length is < the sum of the other 2 sides. A possible longest side-length is 20.

   A) 15   B) 20   C) 25   D) 29

23.
B

24. If $x \square y = (x+y)^2 - 2xy$, then $5 \square 7 = (5+7)^2 - 2 \times 5 \times 7 = 144 - 70 = 74$.

   A) 12   B) 24   C) 35   D) 74

24.
D

25. A square of side-length 4π has perimeter 16π; $C = \pi d$, so $d = 16$.

   A) 2   B) 4   C) 8   D) 16

25.
D

Go on to the next page)))) **8**

26. Since 18 km per 60 minutes = 18/60 km per 1 minute = 0.3 km per 60 seconds, and 0.3 km = 300 m, he runs 300 m in 60 seconds, or 300/60 = 5 m in 1 second. A) 5 B) 6 C) 10 D) 18	26. A
27. -5×30 = -150, 5×20 = 100, and 11×14 = 154. A) -150 B) -30 C) 100 D) 154	27. B
28. Since 1000/20 = 50, 50 are multiples of 4 and 5. Since 1000/60 = 16.666 . . . , 16 are also multiples of 6; 50−16 = 34. A) 34 B) 42 C) 50 D) 58	28. A
29. $\frac{3}{5}:6 = (5\times\frac{3}{5}):(5\times6) = 3:30 = 1:10 = 8:80.$ A) $\frac{20}{9}$ B) $\frac{9}{5}$ C) 24 D) 80	29. D
30. If the average of these integers is 5, then their sum is 15, and the greatest possible value of the sum of their squares is $1^2+1^2+13^2 = 171.$ A) 107 B) 149 C) 171 D) 197	30. C
31. Suppose Cody walked 10 km in 2 hrs. yesterday. Then today she wants to walk 15 km in 1 hr. Since her rate yesterday was 5 km per hr. and her rate today is 15 km per hr., that's a 200% increase. A) 200% B) 300% C) 400% D) 500%	31. A
32. $9^{18} - 3^{32} = 3^{36} - 3^{32} = 3^{32}\times(3^4 - 1) = 3^{32}\times80 = 3^{32}\times2^4\times5.$ A) 5 B) 17 C) 19 D) 31	32. A
33. $3\times6\times9\times12\times15\times18 = 2^4\times3^8\times5$; the factors that are perfect squares are $2^2, 2^4, 3^2, 3^4, 3^6, 3^8, 2^23^2, 2^23^4, 2^23^6, 2^23^8, 2^43^2, 2^43^4, 2^43^6,$ and $2^43^8.$ A) 15 B) 14 C) 7 D) 6	33. B
34. Whatever box Bette checks 1st, the probs. are 2/3 that she checks a different one on the 2nd form and 1/3 that the 3rd form differs from the first two. So the final prob. is 2/3 × 1/3 = 2/9. A) $\frac{1}{4}$ B) $\frac{1}{3}$ C) $\frac{2}{9}$ D) $\frac{3}{10}$	34. C
35. Each number in the sequence 105, 112, 119, . . . , is a multiple of 7, and each number in the sequence 107, 114, 121, . . . , is 2 more than a multiple of 7. Since 2137 is 2 more than a multiple of 7, it may appear in the sequence. A) 1296 B) 1648 C) 2137 D) 2818	35. C

The end of the contest ✍ **8**

Visit our Web site at http://www.mathleague.com

Math League Press, P.O. Box 17, Tenafly, New Jersey 07670-0017

Information & Solutions

Tuesday, February 18 or 25, 2014

8

Contest Information

- **Solutions**   Turn the page for detailed contest solutions (written in the question boxes) and letter answers (written in the *Answer Column* to the right of each question).

- **Scores**   Please remember that *this is a contest, and not a test*—there is no "passing" or "failing" score. Few students score as high as 28 points (80% correct); students with half that, 14 points, *deserve commendation!*

- **Answers and Rating Scales**   Turn to page 144 for the letter answers to each question and the rating scale for this contest.

1. No even number can be written as the product of two odd integers. Since 11 is the product of 1 and 11, Skip may have run 11 kilometers.

   A) 10   B) 11   C) 12   D) 14

   1.
   B

2. $250 + (450 + 650 + 850) = (450 + 650 + 850) + 250.$

   A) 50   B) 250   C) 550   D) 1050

   2.
   B

3. The reciprocal of 2 + the reciprocal of 8 = 1/2 + 1/8 = 4/8 + 1/8 = 5/8 = 5 × 1/8 = 5 times the reciprocal of 8.

   A) 2   B) 6   C) 8   D) 10

   3.
   C

4. Since 0.0449 is closer to 0.04 than 0.05, it rounds to 0.04.

   A) 0.04   B) 0.045   C) 0.05   D) 0.055

   4.
   A

5. The sum of the angle-measures of a triangle is 180°, so the two largest angles must each be less than 90°.

   A) isosceles   B) equilateral   C) acute   D) right

   5.
   D

6. $\dfrac{6}{10} = \dfrac{3}{5} = \dfrac{9}{15}.$

   A) 9   B) 11   C) 12   D) 18

   6.
   A

7. I have equal numbers of nickels, dimes, and quarters. One coin of each value is worth $0.40; $10÷$0.40 = 25, so I can have 24 of each.

   A) 20   B) 24   C) 25   D) 29

   7.
   B

8. Twelve hours after 10 A.M. is 10 P.M.; two hours earlier is 8 P.M.

   A) 8 A.M.   B) 10 A.M.   C) 6 P.M.   D) 8 P.M.

   8.
   D

9. The product of the three smallest prime numbers divided by the sum of these three prime numbers is $(2 \times 3 \times 5) \div (2 + 3 + 5) = 30 \div 10 = 3.$

   A) $\dfrac{6}{5}$ B) 1   C) $\dfrac{5}{3}$ D) 3

   9.
   D

10. Keep doubling until you exceed 1000: 2, 4, 8, 16, 32, 64, 128, 256, 512, 1024. It is 10 days after Sunday when the bell first rang more than 1000 times; 10 days after Sunday is a Wednesday.

    A) Friday B) Sunday C) Tuesday D) Wednesday

    10.
    D

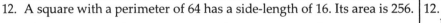

11. The ratio of boys to girls is 4:5. The number of boys is 4/5×60 = 48, and 60 − 48 = 12.

    A) 12   B) 15   C) 18   D) 21

    11.
    A

12. A square with a perimeter of 64 has a side-length of 16. Its area is 256.

    A) 32   B) 64   C) 144   D) 256

    12.
    D

Go on to the next page))))➤ **8**

13. Since $\frac{1}{6}$ of 60 = 10 and this is 5 less than $\frac{1}{4}$ of 60, Sue and Lou do 60 stretches.  A) 120 B) 60 C) 29 D) 24	13. B
14. Rewrite as $(2^5)^{1000}$, $(3^4)^{1000}$, $(4^3)^{1000}$, and $(5^2)^{1000}$. We have $3^4 > 4^3 > 2^5 > 5^2$. A) 2^{5000} B) 3^{4000} C) 4^{3000} D) 5^{2000}	14. B
15. $(5 \times 5) + (5 \div 5) - 5 = 21$; $5 - (5 \div 5) + (5 \times 5) = 29$. Finally, $29 - 21 = 8$. A) 0 B) 8 C) 15 D) 24	15. B
16. 0.25% of 50% of 1600 = $0.0025 \times 0.5 \times 1600 = 2$. A) 2 B) 40 C) 100 D) 200	16. A
17. All primes greater than 2 are odd. Since the sum is odd, one addend is 2. A) 2 B) 3 C) 5 D) 7	17. A
18. If 2 sides of an isosceles triangle are 10 and 25, its perimeter is 10+25+25. A) 45 B) 60 C) 70 D) 75	18. B
19. Out of 7 acotrs, I choose one as Hamlet and another as Othello. These two roles may be chosen in $7 \times 6 = 42$ different ways. A) 13 B) 21 C) 42 D) 49	19. C
20. As shown, each of the two remaining angles measures 120° since each linear pair equals 180°. A) 40° B) 60° C) 90° D) 120°	20. D
21. Since 1 m = 100 cm, the big bottle is 200 cm tall. Since 2 cm on the big bottle equal 1 mm on the model, the model is 100 mm tall. Finally, 100 mm = 0.1 m. A) 0.02 m B) 0.1 m C) 0.2 m D) 1 m	21. B
22. The probability of an event cannot be more than 1. A) 0.02 B) $\frac{3}{\pi}$ C) $\frac{3}{5}$ D) $\frac{7}{6}$	22. D
23. $\frac{6}{5} \div \frac{4}{5} = 6 \div 4 = 1.5 = 150\%$.  A) 150% B) 80% C) 66% D) 40%	23. A
24. Since $36:24 = 3:2 = 54:36$, 36 splikes = 54 splorks. A) 12 B) 24 C) 48 D) 54	24. D
25. The sum of these integers is at least $32 + 34 + 36 + 38 + 40 + 42 + 44 + 46 = 312$. A) 240 B) 256 C) 276 D) 312	25. D

Go on to the next page))))⟶ **8**

26. The ones digits of powers of 8 repeat in a cycle of 8, 4, 2, 6, 8, 4, 2, 6, ... The ones digit of the weight in kg could be 6. A) 0 B) 3 C) 6 D) 9	26. C
27. As shown, only choice D is not a product of a divisor of 24 and a divisor of 35. A) 1×1 B) 6×7 C) 8×7 D) 6×11	27. D
28. The sum of the dimensions is 40÷2 = 20. Its dimensions are 16 × 4, and its area is 64. A) 100 B) 64 C) 40 D) 24	28. B
29. Her average score for 6 tests was 82. So her total was 6×82 = 492. Adding 2×98, her total for 8 tests was 688. Her average score was 86. A) 86 B) 88 C) 90 D) 94	29. A
30. From 1 to 99 there are 9; in every 100 #s after there are 19. Include 1000. A) 162 B) 171 C) 180 D) 181	30. D
31. As shown, there are always 16 nonoverlapping regions. There cannot be fewer regions since no three diagonals of a pentagon can intersect at a common point. A) 18 B) 16 C) 15 D) 11	31. B
32. Written as a fraction, the remainder is 18/100 = 9/50. Therefore, the remainder could be any multiple of 9. A) 12 B) 24 C) 36 D) 48	32. C
33. The least common multiple of 2, 3, 4, 5, 6, 7, 8, or 9 is 2520. When 2521 is divided by 2, 3, 4, 5, 6, 7, 8, or 9, the remainder must be 1. A) 2 and 1000 B) 1000 and 2000 C) 2000 and 3000 D) 3000 and 4000	33. C
34. If Mr. Zilch's pocket was not leaking, it would have taken 18 minutes to fill his half-full pocket. In 9 minutes, it would have been 3/4 full. The hole must have been able to empty a 3/4 full pocket in 9 minutes. At that rate, the hole would have emptied his full pocket in 12 minutes. A) 12 B) 18 C) 36 D) 72	34. A
35. We have 228 g of pure gold in 1800 g of ore; this is 12⅔% gold. Since 12⅔ is 8/3 more than 10 and 7/3 less than 15, the ratio of my ore to yours is 7/3:8/3 = 7:8, so 7/15 of the 1800 g is my ore. A) 820 B) 840 C) 880 D) 960	35. B

The end of the contest **8**

Information & Solutions

Tuesday, February 17 or 24, 2015

8

Contest Information

- **Solutions**   Turn the page for detailed contest solutions (written in the question boxes) and letter answers (written in the *Answer Column* to the right of each question).

- **Scores**   Please remember that *this is a contest, and not a test*—there is no "passing" or "failing" score. Few students score as high as 28 points (80% correct); students with half that, 14 points, *deserve commendation!*

- **Answers and Rating Scales**   Turn to page 146 for the letter answers to each question and the rating scale for this contest.

1. $2014 + 2015 = (1014 + 1000) + (1015 + 1000) = 1014 + 1015 + (1000 + 1000)$.

   A) 200   B) 1000   C) 1200   D) 2000

   1.
   D

2. The number of houses that Sam demolished is the product of consecutive integers. Since $72 = 8 \times 9$, Sam may have demolished 72 houses.

   A) 54   B) 63   C) 72   D) 81

   2.
   C

3. The product of 5 000 000 000 and 8 000 000 000 is 40 followed by 18 0s. That's 20 digits.

   A) 20   B) 19   C) 11   D) 10

   3.
   A

4. Since $380 = 95 \times 4 = 380 \times 1$, the desired sum is $95 + 380 = 475$.

   A) 759   B) 475   C) 285   D) 171

   4.
   B

5. Find the choice that, when multiplied by 4, yields a perfect square. Since $4 \times 1 = 4 = 2 \times 2$, choice A is correct.

   A) 1   B) 2   C) 3   D) 5

   5.
   A

6. My sandwich cost $10 \times 25¢ + 10 \times 10¢ + 10 \times 5¢ = 400¢ = \$4.00$. I paid for it with a \$20 bill. I got $\$20.00 - \$4.00 = \$16.00$ back in change.

   A) \$8.00   B) \$10.00   C) \$12.00   D) \$16.00

   6.
   D

7. 600 seconds = 10 minutes; the time is 12:10 A.M.

   A) 12:10 P.M.   B) 10:00 P.M.   C) 12:10 A.M.   D) 10:00 A.M.

   7.
   C

8. $(32 \div 2) \times 4 - 6 = 16 \times 4 - 6 = 64 - 6 = 58$.

   A) -8   B) -2   C) 16   D) 58

   8.
   D

9. $2 + 3 + 5 + 7 + 11 + 13 + 17 + 19 = 77$.

   A) 17   B) 59   C) 77   D) 89

   9.
   C

10. Deborah Harried had only two breaks, each for a whole number of minutes. If the product of the two whole numbers is prime, one number must be 1 and the other a prime. The numbers could be 1 and 11. Their sum is $1 + 11 = 12$.

    A) 5   B) 12   C) 13   D) 19

    10.
    B

11. $\dfrac{5+5}{8+8} = \dfrac{10}{16} = \dfrac{5}{8} + 0$.

    A) 0   B) $\dfrac{5}{16}$ C) $\dfrac{5}{8}$ D) 1

    11.
    A

12. One angle has measure 90°. The other 2 angles must have measures of 25° and 65° since the sum of the measures of all 3 angles is 180°.

    A) 10°   B) 25°   C) 40°   D) 50°

    12.
    B

Go on to the next page ⟫➤ **8**

13. Since choice A is negative, it is least. A) -100^2 B) $(-49)^2$ C) 19^3 D) $(0.5)^4$	13. A
14. Merino now earns $640 per week. This is 80% of what he earned last week. Last week he earned $640 ÷ 0.80 = $800. Similarly, before the cuts, Merino earned $800 ÷ 0.80 = $1000. A) 896.00 B) 921.60 C) 1000.00 D) 1066.67	14. C
15. The average of 6 6's and 3 12's is (36 + 36) ÷ 9. A) 6 B) 8 C) 8.5 D) 9	15. B
16. The sum of the tenths and hundreds digits of 321.123 is 1 + 3 = 4. A) 2 B) 3 C) 4 D) 5	16. C
17. Since $7^{77} + 7^7 + 7$ is divisible by 7, the remainder is 0. A) 0 B) 1 C) 3 D) 4	17. A
18. $\left(-\dfrac{6}{5}\right) \times \left(-\dfrac{5}{4}\right) \times \left(-\dfrac{4}{3}\right) \times \left(-\dfrac{3}{2}\right) \times \left(-\dfrac{2}{1}\right) \times \left(-\dfrac{1}{6}\right) = \left(\dfrac{6\times5\times4\times3\times2\times1}{720}\right).$ A) -720 B) -1 C) 1 D) 720	18. D
19. As shown below, only choice B cannot be written as such a sum. A) 2.0 = 1 + 1 B) 2.8 C) 4.25 = 4 + 1/4 D) 8.125 = 8 + 1/8	19. B
20. Jen has at least 5 pennies. Adding these pennies to 1 quarter and 2 nickels, she has 40¢. The $1.60 remaining could consist of 16 dimes. A) 13 B) 14 C) 15 D) 16	20. D
21. Tom spent 12 hours in the sun the last 4 days for an average of 3 hours per day. His average for 6 days is twice this or 6 hours per day. He spent 6 × 6 = 36 hours in the sun in the last 6 days. A) 12 B) 24 C) 36 D) 48	21. C
22. 5×4 + 5×8 + 5×12 + 5×16 + 5×20 = (4+8+12+16+20)×5. A) 4 B) 5 C) 25 D) 5^5	22. B
23. 30(2◊1) = 30(2×2 − 1) = 3◊3 = 2×3 − 3 = 3. A) 3 B) 5 C) 7 D) 9	23. A
24. The area is half the product of the legs, so this product is 120. The area of the square is also 120. A) 30 B) 60 C) 120 D) 225	24. C
25. Using 2, 3, and 5, the divisors are 1, 2, 3, 5, 6, 10, 15, and 30. A) 3 B) 6 C) 7 D) 8	25. D

Go on to the next page))▶ **8**

26. At work I asked each person who wanted ice cream to raise a hand. If 10% of 100% of 1000% of the 30 people at work raised hands, $0.1 \times 1 \times 10 \times 30 = 30$ people raised hands.

   A) 3   B) 10   C) 15   D) 30

26.

D

27. If x has 6 factors, pairs of factors have a product of x. The product of the 3 pairs is $x \times x \times x$.

   A) x^3 B) x^4 C) x^6 D) x^7

27.

A

28. The sum of the 8 consecutive integers from -3 to 4 is 4.

   A) 0   B) 2   C) 4   D) 8

28.

C

29. The squares of 1 and -1 are both 1, and one-fourth of 1 is less than 1. The square of 0 is 0, and one-fourth of 0 is also less than 1.

   A) 1   B) 2   C) 3   D) 4

29.

C

30. If the measures of 2 angles in this triangle are 40 and 80, the 3rd angle must have measure 40 or 80. The sum of the measures is not 180.

   A) 40, 80   B) 45, 90   C) 50, 65   D) 60, 60

30.

A

31. The only such primes are 113 and 127. Their difference is 14.

   A) 2   B) 3   C) 8   D) 14

31.

D

32. $3 \times 2^{96} = (2+1) \times 2^{96} = (2 \times 2^{96}) + (1 \times 2^{96}) = 2^{97} + 2^{96}$.

   A) $2^{97} + 2$ B) $2^{97} + 2^{96}$ C) $6^{32} + 6^{32}$ D) 6^{96}

32.

B

33. I got 90% of my math questions correct. For every 10 questions on this test, I got 9 correct. Thus, for every 20 questions, I got 18 correct. There must be 20 more questions on my math test than on my history test.

   A) 18   B) 20   C) 36   D) 180

33.

B

34. We need to calculate $2 \times (3 + 6 + \ldots + 30) + 4 \times (3 + 6 + \ldots + 30) + \ldots + 20 \times (3 + 6 + \ldots + 30)$. This calculation is equivalent to $(2 + 4 + \ldots + 20) \times (3 + 6 + \ldots + 30) = (110) \times (165) = 18\,150$.

   A) 18150   B) 108900
   C) 217800   D) 653400

34.

A

35. There are 2 ways to pick one line and 10 ways to pick 2 dots on it. There are 5 ways to choose 1 dot on the 2nd line. That's $2 \times 10 \times 5 = 100$ triangles.

   A) 80   B) 90   C) 100   D) 110

35.

C

The end of the contest **8**

Visit our Web site at http://www.mathleague.com

Information & Solutions

Tuesday, February 16 or 23, 2016

8

Contest Information

- **Solutions** Turn the page for detailed contest solutions (written in the question boxes) and letter answers (written in the *Answer Column* to the right of each question).

- **Scores** Please remember that *this is a contest, and not a test*—there is no "passing" or "failing" score. Few students score as high as 28 points (80% correct); students with half that, 14 points, *deserve commendation!*

- **Answers and Rating Scales** Turn to page 147 for the letter answers to each question and the rating scale for this contest.

Copyright © 2016 by Mathematics Leagues Inc.

				Answers
1.	Since the ones digit of 2016 is neither 0 nor 5, it is not divisible by 5.			1.
	A) 4 B) 5 C) 6 D) 7			B
2.	Wally has chewed up a total of 10×750 = 7500 grams of logs. This is $7500 \div 1000$ = 7.5 kilograms.			2.
	A) 0.075 B) 0.75 C) 7.5 D) 75			C
3.	$(12 \div 6) + (3 \times 0) - 3 = 2 + 0 - 3 = -1$.			3.
	A) -3 B) -1 C) 1 D) 3			B
4.	20% of 0.3% of 40 000 = $0.20 \times 0.003 \times 40\,000$.			4.
	A) 24 B) 240 C) 2400 D) 24 000			A
5.	The mean is $(10 + 20 + 30 + 30 + 40 + 50) \div 6 = 30$. The median and the mode are both 30. The range is $50 - 10 = 40$. The range is greatest.			5.
	A) mean B) median C) range D) mode			C
6.	2013 and 2016 are multiples of 3, and 2015 is a multiple of 5.			6.
	A) 2016 B) 2015 C) 2013 D) 2011			D
7.	This is the sum of two odd and two even numbers. The sum is even.			7.
	A) 2 B) 3 C) 4 D) 5			A
8.	After choosing one vertex of the cube, we see that only 1 out of the 7 remaining vertices can be chosen. Thus the answer is 2.			8.
	A) 1 B) 2 C) 3 D) 4			B
9.	If 12 345 is divided by 100, the result is 123.45. The hundreds digit is 1 and the tenths digit is 4. Their sum is 5.			9.
	A) 3 B) 5 C) 7 D) 9			B
10.	Bob's bricklaying crew lays 10, 20, 40, 80, 160, 320, 640 and 1280 bricks during each of the 8 hours, respectively. Together, the crew lays a total of $10 + 20 + 40 + 80 + 160 + 320 + 640 + 1280 = 2550$ bricks.			10.
	A) 280 B) 360 C) 1280 D) 2550			D
11.	The g.c.f of 80 and 210 is 10, which has 4 positive integer factors.			11.
	A) 2 B) 3 C) 4 D) 5			C
12.	The cost of a bat and a ball, $34.10, is the same as the cost of two balls plus $20. The cost of a ball is $(\$34.10 - \$20) \div 2 = \$7.05$.			12.
	A) 7.05 B) 7.10 C) 27.05 D) 27.10			A

Go on to the next page ⟫➡ **8**

13. The total value of the coins, in cents, is $1000 \times 25 + 2000 \times 10 + 3000 \times 5 + 4000 \times 1 = 64000$. The average value of 1 coin is $64000 \div 10000 = 6.4$¢. A) 3.2¢ B) 32¢ C) 6.4¢ D) 64¢	13. C
14. As powers of 0.9 get larger, powers get closer to 0. A) 0 B) 0.3 C) 0.9 D) 1	14. A
15. The price of the book after a 30% increase was $\$20 \times (1 + 0.3) = \$26$. The 30% discount from the new price is $\$26 \times (1 - 0.3) = \$18.20$. A) \$15.00 B) \$18.20 C) \$20.00 D) \$23.80	15. B
16. The largest angle's measure is between 90° and 180°. Hence 30° < smallest angle < 60°. The angles could be 35°, 40°, and 105°. A) 100° B) 80° C) 60° D) 40°	16. D
17. There are 49 positive multiple of 2 less than 100. Of these, 24 num- bers are divisible by 4. Thus the answer is 24/49. A) $\dfrac{1}{4}$ B) $\dfrac{11}{24}$ C) $\dfrac{24}{49}$ D) $\dfrac{1}{2}$	17. C
18. The product of the integers from 1 to 9 has 0 as its ones digit, thus so will the product of the integers from 1 000 001 through 1 000 009. A) 0 B) 1 C) 4 D) 5	18. A
19. The only such integers are 1 and –1. A) 0 B) 1 C) 2 D) 3	19. C
20. The ones digits of 17^{18} and 19^{20} are 9 and 1 respectively. A) 0 B) 1 C) 8 D) 9	20. A
21. The barrel will be 1/32 full on Day 2, 1/16 full on Day 3, 1/8 full on Day 4, 1/4 full on Day 5, and 1/2 full on Day 6. A) 5 B) 6 C) 7 D) 8	21. B
22. 159 360 seconds $\div$ 60 sec/min = 2656 min = 44 hours and 16 minutes. A) 8:08 AM B) 8:16 AM C) 8:08 PM D) 8:16 PM	22. D
23. $2^3 \times 3^4 \times 5^4 = 2^2 \times 3^3 \times 5^3 \times (2 \times 3 \times 5)$. A) 15 B) 30 C) 60 D) 120	23. B
24. $5^{336} \times 25^{336} \times 125^{336} = 5^{336} \times 5^{672} \times 5^{1008} = 5^{2016}$. A) 1008 B) 1344 C) 1680 D) 2016	24. D
25. $2@(3@4) = 2@(3 \times 4 - 3 - 4) = 2@5 = 2 \times 5 - 2 - 5 = 3$. A) -1 B) 1 C) 3 D) 10	25. C

Go on to the next page))))▶ **8**

26. Baron flies 2^{16} m, 2^{17} m, and 2^{18} m on the 17th, 18th, and 19th days, respectively. Together, he flies a total of $2^{16} + 2^{17} + 2^{18} = (1 \times 2^{16}) + (2 \times 2^{16}) + (4 \times 2^{16}) = 7 \times 2^{16}$ m.

A) 7×2^{16} B) 3×2^{18} C) 2^{19} D) 2^{20}

26.

A

27. The sum of any two sides is greater than the third side. The third side must be greater than $65 - 35 = 30$ and less than $65 + 35 = 100$.

A) 29   B) 69   C) 70   D) 71

27.

B

28. If there are 24 peas, then there are 20 parsnips, 30 peppers, and 9 potatoes. The ratio of potatoes to peppers is $9:30 = 3:10$.

A) $3:10$ B) $4:5$ C) $5:4$ D) $10:3$

28.

A

29. At this farm, 80% of the eggs weren't large, and $2\% \times 80\% = 0.016$ of the eggs were incorrectly labeled large. Since that represents 50 eggs, a total of $50 \div 0.016 = 3125$ eggs were laid.

A) 2500   B) 3125   C) 6250   D) 50000

29.

B

30. If the square is less than $\dfrac{1}{16}$, then the number is between 0 and $-\dfrac{1}{4}$. Reciprocals of all such numbers are less than -4.

A) less than -4   B) between -4 and 0
C) between 0 and 4   D) greater than 4

30.

A

31. Since $2016 = 2^5 \times 3^2 \times 7$, the product must include not only a 7 but also at least 5 2s and 2 3s. $1 \times 2 \times 3 \times (2^2) \times 5 \times (2 \times 3) \times 7 \times (2^3)$ is the least.

A) 7   B) 8   C) 21   D) 63

31.

B

32. The smaller number must leave a remainder of 0 or 2 when divided by 3. Of the 90 integers from 10 to 99, 60 of them can be the smaller #.

A) $\dfrac{1}{3}$ B) $\dfrac{1}{2}$ C) $\dfrac{3}{5}$ D) $\dfrac{2}{3}$

32.

D

33. Together, Al, Barb, and Cy can do $1/2 + 1/3 + 1/6 = 6/6$ of the work in 1 year. Working together, they can build the bridge in 1 year.

A) 1   B) 1.2   C) 1.6   D) 1.8

33.

A

34. A semicircle of radius 10 cm has area 50π cm². Since 1 cm² $= 100$ mm², 50π cm² $= 5000\pi$ mm².

A) 500π B) 5000π
C) 1000π D) 10000π

34.

B

35. There are 6 ways to choose 2 couples. There are 4 ways to choose 1 couple, and then 12 ways to choose 2 additional people who aren't a couple. The total is $6 + 4 \times 12 = 54$.

A) 16   B) 50   C) 54   D) 60

35.

C

The end of the contest ✍ ◀ **8**

Algebra Course 1 Solutions

2011-2012 through 2015-2016

Information & Solutions

Spring, 2012

Contest Information

A

- **Solutions** Turn the page for detailed contest solutions (written in the question boxes) and letter answers (written in the *Answer Column* to the right of each question).

- **Scores** Please remember that *this is a contest, and not a test*—there is no "passing" or "failing" score. Few students score as high as 24 points (80% correct); students with half that, 12 points, *deserve commendation!*

- **Answers and Rating Scales** Turn to page 148 for the letter answers to each question and the rating scale for this contest.

1. If $x = 2012$ and $y = 2011$, then $(x + y)(x - y) = (2012 + 2011)(1)$. A) $2012 + 2011$ B) $2012 - 2011$ C) 2012^2 D) 2011^2	1. A
2. Let ℓ = the length of the rope. Since $\ell = 2(\dfrac{1}{2r})$, the length of the rope is $\dfrac{1}{r}$. A) r B) $\dfrac{1}{r}$ C) $4r$ D) $\dfrac{1}{4r}$	2. B
3. The points $(3,5)$ and $(13,5)$ are on a horizontal line. The points $(13,5)$ and $(13,13)$ are on a vertical line. Thus $(13,13)$ could be the 3rd vertex. A) $(16,10)$ B) $(8,7)$ C) $(5,5)$ D) $(13,13)$	3. D
4. The roots of $(x - 6)(x + 12) = 0$ are 6 and -12. Their sum is -6. A) -18 B) -6 C) 6 D) 18	4. B
5. Since $(x + y) \div 2 = 5$, $x + y = 10$ and $(x + y)^2 = 10^2 = 100$. A) 25 B) 50 C) 100 D) 400	5. C
6. There are 10 multiples of 7 that are between 700 and 770. Thus there are $s + 10$ multiples greater than 0 and less than 770. A) $s + 7$ B) $s + 9$ C) $s + 10$ D) $s + 11$	6. C
7. $(x+1) - (2-2x) - (x-1) + (2+2x) = x+1-2+2x-x+1+2+2x = 4x+2$. A) 0 B) 2 C) $4x + 2$ D) $2x + 4$	7. C
8. Since $A = \pi r^2$ and $C = 2\pi r$, $A \div C = r/2$. We are told that $r/2 = 4$. Thus, $r = 8$ and $d = 16$. A) 2 B) 4 C) 8 D) 16	8. D
9. $\dfrac{x^3 + x^2}{x} = \dfrac{x^3}{x} + \dfrac{x^2}{x} = x^2 + x$. A) $2x^2$ B) $x^2 + x$ C) $x^3 + x$ D) x^4	9. B
10. Bo is lifting weights at his desk. He does n lifts. If $n^2 - 18n = -81$, $n^2 - 18n + 81 = (n - 9)^2 = 0$, so $n = 9$. A) 9 B) 18 C) 36 D) 81	10. A
11. Let $5r$ = # of red roses and $3r$ = # of yellow roses. Then $5r - 3r = 14$; so $2r = 14$ and $r = 7$. There are $5r = 35$ red roses. A) 12 B) 17 C) 21 D) 35	11. D

Go on to the next page)))▶ **A**

12. The slopes of perpendicular lines are negative reciprocals if neither slope is 0. The slope of $2x - 3y = -9$ is 2/3; the slope of C is -3/2. A) $3x - 4y = -12$ B) $2x - 3y = 12$ C) $3x + 2y = -10$ D) $2x + 3y = 18$	12. C
13. Horace Hippo will wait h hours for his client. If $h^2 - 2h - 15 < 0$, then $(h - 5)(h + 3) < 0$. Thus $-3 < h < 5$, and the largest integral value of h is 4. A) 6 B) 5 C) 4 D) 3	13. C
14. I have $\lvert 3x \rvert = 3\lvert x \rvert$ pencils and you have $\lvert -2x \rvert = 2\lvert x \rvert$ pencils. Together we have $5\lvert x \rvert$ pencils. A) $\lvert x \rvert$ B) x C) $5x$ D) $5\lvert x \rvert$	14. D
15. The roots of $x^2 - 20x + 91 = (x - 7)(x - 13) = 0$ are 7 and 13. The roots of $x^2 - 22x + 117 = (x - 9)(x - 13) = 0$ are 9 and 13. My age must be 13, so the sum of my brother's age and my sister's age is $7 + 9 = 16$. A) 16 B) 20 C) 22 D) 26	15. A
16. If 3 is one solution to $x^2 + 2x + c = 21$, then $3^2 + 2(3) + c = 21$. Solving, $c = 6$, so $x^2 + 2x + 6 = 21$, $x^2 + 2x - 15 = (x + 5)(x - 3) = 0$, and $x = -5, 3$. A) -5 B) -2 C) 2 D) 7	16. A
17. If $x + (x - 1) + \ldots + (x - 8) + (x - 9) = 75$, then $10x - 45 = 75$ and $x = 12$. A) 10 B) 12 C) 15 D) 17	17. B
18. The horizontal line $y = 1$ passes through only quadrants I and II. A) $y = x + 2$ B) $y = 2x - 1$ C) $y = 1$ D) $x = 1$	18. C
19. The average of $x, y,$ and z is 6; their sum is 18. The average of $a, b,$ and c is 4; their sum is 12. Thus $(x + y + z)^2 - (a + b + c)^2 = 18^2 - 12^2$. A) 4 B) 20 C) 36 D) 180	19. D
20. Since n^5 is divisible by n^2, and n^5 is also divisible by n^4, the least common multiple of $n^2, n^4,$ and n^5 is n^5. A) n^2 B) n^5 C) n^{11} D) n^{20}	20. B
21. $2[2(2^3)^4]^5 \div \{2[2(2^5)^4]^3\} = 2[2(2^{12})]^5 \div \{2[2(2^{20})]^3\} = 2^{66} \div 2^{64} = 2^2$. A) 1 B) 2 C) 2^2 D) 2^3	21. C
22. The number, N, of integers between $2x$ and $4x$ is 1 less than the difference between $4x$ and $2x$, so $N = (4x - 2x) - 1 = 2x - 1$. A) x B) $2x - 1$ C) $2x$ D) $2x + 1$	22. B

Go on to the next page))))➡ **A**

119

23. Since 8, 15, and 24 may be written as a product of 2 integers that differ by 2, the first three equations have integral roots.

    A) $k^2 - 2k = 8$ B) $k^2 - 2k = 15$
    C) $k^2 - 2k = 24$ D) $k^2 - 2k = 30$

23.

D

24. Divide both sides of $\frac{4}{x} < 12$ by 4 to get $\frac{1}{x} < 3$.

    If $x = -1$, A and B are false; if $x = 2$, D is false.

    A) $x > 3$ B) $x > \frac{1}{3}$ C) $\frac{1}{x} < 3$ D) $\frac{1}{x} < \frac{1}{3}$

24.

C

25. Since $(x + y)^3 = x^3 + 3x^2y + 3xy^2 + y^3$, $(x + y)^3 = x^3 + y^3 + 3xy(x + y)$. Thus, $a^3 = x^3 + y^3 + 3b(a)$, and $x^3 + y^3 = a^3 - 3ab$.

    A) $a^3 + 3ab$ B) $a^3 - 3ab$ C) $a^3 + b^3$ D) $a^3 - b^3$

25.

B

26. For integers, $y^2 - x^2 = (y + x)(y - x)$ is the product of 2 even integers or 2 odd integers. If both factors are even, it's divisible by 4; $768 = 4 \times 192$.

    A) 386   B) 558   C) 768   D) 970

26.

C

27. If $(n!)^2 - 21(n!) - 72 = 0$, then $(n! + 3)(n! - 24) = 0$ and $n! = 24$. Since $24 = 4 \times 3 \times 2 \times 1$, $n = 4$.

    A) 6   B) 5   C) 4   D) 3

27.

C

28. Since $4y = 6z - 3x = 3(2z - x)$, we can see that y is divisible by 3. Since 285 is divisible by 3, y could be 285.

    A) 285   B) 319   C) 422   D) 500

28.

A

29. Let D = dist. from home to beach. Avg. rate = (total dist./total time), so avg. rate was $2D \div (D/90 + D/110)$. Divide num. and denom. by D. Average rate = $2 \div (1/90 + 1/110) = 2 \div (200/9900) = 99$.

    A) 98   B) 99   C) 100   D) 101

29.

B

30. The roots of $x^2 - cx + 36 = 0$ are in a 4:1 ratio. Since their product is 36, they are 3 and 12 or -3 and -12. Thus $c = 15$ or -15.

    A) -225   B) -36   C) 15   D) 120

30.

A

The end of the contest ✍ **A**

Visit our Web site at http://www.mathleague.com

Information & Solutions

Spring, 2013

Contest Information

- **Solutions** Turn the page for detailed contest solutions (written in the question boxes) and letter answers (written in the *Answer Column* to the right of each question).

- **Scores** Please remember that *this is a contest, and not a test*—there is no "passing" or "failing" score. Few students score as high as 24 points (80% correct); students with half that, 12 points, *deserve commendation!*

- **Answers and Rating Scales** Turn to page 149 for the letter answers to each question and the rating scale for this contest.

1. If $x = 2013$, then $(x - 2012)^{(x - 2013)} = (2013 - 2012)^{(2013 - 2013)} = 1^0 = 1$.

   A) 0   B) 1   C) 2   D) 10

1.

B

2. If $a = 5$, then $4a^3 - 3a^2 + 2a - 1 = 4(5)^3 - 3(5)^2 + 2(5) - 1 = 500 - 75 + 10 - 1$.

   A) 39   B) 125   C) 434   D) 586

2.

C

3. Fred and Ginger danced for $\dfrac{2013}{x}$ hours last year. Since 2013 is not divisible by 13, x *cannot* be 13.

   A) 3   B) 11   C) 13   D) 61

3.

C

4. We may rewrite $x^2 - 4x - 12$ as $(x - 6)(x + 2)$, so $x + 2$ is a factor.

   A) $x + 2$ B) $x - 2$ C) x D) $x - 8$

4.

A

5. $2^{400} + 2^{400} = 2(2^{400}) = (2^1)(2^{400}) = 2^{400 + 1} = 2^{401}$.

   A) 2^{401} B) 2^{800} C) 4^{400} D) 4^{800}

5.

A

6. If $\dfrac{p}{q} = \dfrac{2}{3}$, then $\dfrac{-p}{-q} = \dfrac{-2}{-3} = \dfrac{2}{3}$

   A) $-\dfrac{2}{3}$ B) $\dfrac{-2}{3}$ C) $\dfrac{2}{-3}$ D) $\dfrac{2}{3}$

6.

D

7. The number of 5 kg weights and 10 kg weights I have is $4w$ and $2w$, respectively. Hence, $5(4w) + 10(2w) = 200$, so $40w = 200$ and $w = 5$.

   A) 4   B) 5   C) 10   D) 20

7.

B

8. $(3x^3 - 4x^2) + (2x^2 - 3x) - (3x^3 - 4) = 3x^3 - 4x^2 + 2x^2 - 3x - 3x^3 + 4 = -2x^2 - 3x + 4$.

   A) $2x^2 - 3x - 4$ B) $2x^2 - 3x + 4$ C) $-2x^2 - 3x - 4$ D) $-2x^2 - 3x + 4$

8.

D

9. Since $3x + 10 = (3x - 4) + 14$, $3x + 10$ is odd. (Odd # + 14 = odd #.)

   A) positive   B) prime   C) odd   D) even

9.

C

10. Yesterday the phone rang at 4 PM or later 80% of the time it rang, and it rang 50 times before 4 PM. Those 50 rings are 20% of all the rings. Thus, the phone rang 250 times yesterday.

   A) 200   B) 250   C) 300   D) 400

10.

B

11. Let the ages of the 5 trees be $t, t - 2, t - 4, t - 6, t - 8$. Then $t + (t - 2) + (t - 4) + (t - 6) + (t - 8) = 4440$. Thus, $5t - 20 = 4440$, and $t = 892$.

   A) 884   B) 888   C) 890   D) 892

11.

D

Go on to the next page ⟫➡ **A**

12. A line that passes through the points (p,q) and $(2p,3q)$ has slope $(3q-q)/(2p-p) = 2q/p$. The slope between (p,q) and $(3p,5q)$ is also $2q/p$. A) $(3p,4q)$ B) $(3p,5q)$ C) $(4p,6q)$ D) $(4p,8q)$	12. B
13. The multiples of 3 between -9 and 12 include 0, so their product is 0. A) -314 928 B) -2916 C) 0 D) 2916	13. C
14. Of children born at the maternity ward yesterday, the ratio of boys to girls was $3x:4y = 5:6$. Thus, $18x = 20y$ or $9x = 10y$. Hence, $x:y = 10:9$. A) 10:9 B) 24:15 C) 15:24 D) 4:5	14. A
15. $$\frac{\left(x^{200}\right)^{400}}{\left(x^{100}\right)^{200}} = \frac{x^{80\,000}}{x^{20\,000}} = x^{60\,000}.$$ A) x^4 B) x^6 C) $x^{40\,000}$ D) $x^{60\,000}$	15. D
16. If the average of x, y, and z is 16, their sum is $3(16) = 48$. If the average of x and y is 12, their sum is $2(12) = 24$. Hence $z = 48-24 = 24$. A) 4 B) 14 C) 20 D) 24	16. D
17. Both $6n^8$ and $10n^{12}$ are factors of $30n^{12}$, the lcm. A) $2n^8$ B) $30n^{12}$ C) $30n^{24}$ D) $60n^{96}$	17. B
18. If the perim. is 64, each side has length 16. By Pythag. Th., a diameter is $16\sqrt{2}$. The area is $(8\sqrt{2})^2\pi = 128\pi$. A) 16π B) 32π C) 64π D) 128π	18. D
19. Since $(x-y)^2 = 3^2$, $x^2 + y^2 - 2xy = 9$. Hence $485 - 2xy = 9$, and $xy = 238$. A) 162 B) 238 C) 482 D) 3880	19. B
20. The roots of $(x-1)(x+2)(x-3)\times\ldots\times$ $(x-19)(x+20)(x-21) = 0$ are 1, -2, 3, -4, ..., 19, -20, and 21. Their sum is $(1-2) + (3-4) + \ldots$ $+ (19-20) + 21 = -10 + 21 = 11$. A) 10 B) 11 C) 21 D) 31	20. B
21. $\left|4x\right| + 4\left|-x\right| = 4\left|x\right| + 4\left|x\right| = 8\left|x\right|$. A) 0 B) 8 C) $8\left|x\right|$ D) $4\left|4x\right|$	21. C
22. $\sqrt{36^{64}} = \sqrt{\left(36^{32}\right)\left(36^{32}\right)} = 36^{32}$. A) 6^8 B) 6^{32} C) 36^8 D) 36^{32}	22. D

Go on to the next page))))➤ **A**

23. If $(x-2)^2 = 1600$, $x - 2 = \pm40$. Thus $x = 42$ or -38, and $x - 4 = 38$ or -42.

    A) -42   B) -34   C) 34   D) 36

23.

A

24. Since the prime factorization of 260 is (2)(2)(5)(13), the least possible value of x is 13.

    A) 10   B) 13   C) 26   D) 30

24.

B

25. Avg. speed = (total dist./total time), so Don Q's avg. speed is $(60 + 60)/[60/(3r) + 60/(6r)] = 120/(30/r) = 4r$.

    A) 4r B) 4.5r C) 5r D) 5.5r

25.

A

26. If the integer is $10t + u$, then the difference be-between this integer and the integer with the digits reversed is $(10t + u) - (10u + t) = 9t - 9u = 36$. Dividing by 9, $t - u = 4$.

    A) 4   B) 6   C) 8   D) 9

26.

A

27. My sister has s dollars, and I have d dollars more than she has. If together we have a total of t dollars, then $s + (s + d) = t$, so $2s = t - d$ and $s = (t - d)/2$.

    A) $t - 2d$ B) $\dfrac{t}{2} - d$ C) $t - \dfrac{d}{2}$ D) $\dfrac{t-d}{2}$

27.

D

28. Choice D is the product of 3 consecutive integers, so it's divisible by 3.

    A) $x(x-3)(x-6)$ B) $x(x+3)(x-3)$ C) $x(x+7)(x-2)$ D) $x(x+1)(x-1)$

28.

D

29.

The expression $\dfrac{2x+1}{3x-3}$ becomes $\dfrac{2(\frac{4}{x})+1}{3(\frac{4}{x})-3} = \dfrac{\frac{8}{x}+1}{\frac{12}{x}-3} = \dfrac{8+x}{12-3x}$.

    A) $\dfrac{2x+1}{3x-3}$ B) $\dfrac{3x-3}{2x+1}$ C) $\dfrac{8+x}{12-3x}$ D) $\dfrac{12x-3}{8x+1}$

29.

C

30. The inequality is true if $x = -3$ or -4. If $x < -4$ or $-3 < x < 5$, it is false. If $x = 6$ or 7, it is true.

    $\dfrac{(x+3)(x+4)}{x-5} \geq 0$.

    My car has 4 passengers.

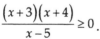

    A) 2   B) 3   C) 4   D) 5

30.

C

The end of the contest **A**

Visit our Web site at http://www.mathleague.com

Information & Solutions

Spring, 2014

Contest Information

- **Solutions**   Turn the page for detailed contest solutions (written in the question boxes) and letter answers (written in the *Answer Column* to the right of each question).

- **Scores**   Please remember that *this is a contest, and not a test* — there is no "passing" or "failing" score. Few students score as high as 24 points (80% correct); students with half that, 12 points, *deserve commendation!*

- **Answers and Rating Scales**   Turn to page 150 for the letter answers to each question and the rating scale for this contest.

1. If $x = 3$, $2014x^2 - 2014x + 2014 = 2014(x^2 - x + 1) = 2014(9 - 3 + 1)$. A) 2014 B) 2014×3 C) 2014×6 D) 2014×7	1. D
2. If x is an integer, then the least integral value of $\dfrac{6}{x}$ is $\dfrac{6}{-1} = -6$. A) -6 B) -3 C) -1 D) 1	2. A
3. Max Peters painted p faces with 2 eyes each for a subtotal of $2p$ eyes. He painted one additional face with only 1 eye. He painted a total of $2p + 1$ eyes. A) $p^2 + 1$ B) $2(p + 1)$ C) $2p + 1$ D) $p + 3$	3. C
4. $(200^8)(200^9)(200^0) = 200^{(8 + 9 + 0)} = 200^{17}$. A) 200^{72} B) 200^{17} C) 200^0 D) 0	4. B
5. $x^2 + xy = x(x + y) = 20$ and $x + y = 10$; thus $x(10) = 20$ and $x = 2$. A) 2 B) 5 C) 10 D) 30	5. A
6. Since 24 is a factor of 48, the l.c.m. of 24 and 48 is 48. A) 2 B) 48 C) 96 D) 1152	6. B
7. The reciprocal of $\sqrt{3}$ is $\dfrac{1}{\sqrt{3}} = \dfrac{\sqrt{3}}{3}$. A) $\sqrt{3}$ B) 3 C) $\dfrac{\sqrt{3}}{3}$ D) $\dfrac{3}{\sqrt{3}}$	7. C
8. If 25% of the students are wearing boots, then the ratio of students wearing boots to students not wearing boots is 25:75 = 1:3. A) 25:100 B) 75:100 C) 1:4 D) 1:3	8. D
9. The positive integers that satisfy $|x - 5| < 3$ are 7, 6, 5, 4, and 3. A) 5 B) 7 C) 8 D) 10	9. A
10. Mr. Rorke flies to a private island in $x - 20$ minutes and flies back in $x - 10$ minutes. Both flights together take 76 minutes. Thus $(x - 20) + (x - 10) = 76$, $x = 53$, and $x - 15 = 38$. A) 38 B) 53 C) 61 D) 400	10. A
11. The sum of the roots of $x^2 - 6x - 432 = 0$ is the opposite of the coefficient of x divided by the coefficient of x^2. A) 2 B) 6 C) 18 D) 42	11. B

Go on to the next page)))》 **A**

12. The slopes (if defined) of 2 $\perp$ lines are negative reciprocals.				12. C
A) 1	B) 4	C) -1	D) -4	

13. Since $(x-2)(x+2)(x-1)(x+1)(x) = x(x^2-4)(x^2-1) = x^5 - 5x^3 + 4x$, my polynomial has exactly 3 terms.	13. D
A) 6 B) 5 C) 4 D) 3	

14. The Fergusons are counting pairs of lovebirds from a hot air balloon. Over 5 days they see totals of n, $n+1$, $n+2$, $n+3$, and $n+4$ pairs, for a total of 360 birds. Hence $2(n+n+1+n+2+n+3+n+4) = 360$, so $n = 34$.	14. A
A) 34 B) 35 C) 70 D) 140	

15. Speedy the snail moves $x/60$ cm per minute. In $10y$ minutes, Speedy moves $10y(x/60) = xy/6$ cm.	15. C
A) $\dfrac{x}{600y}$ B) $6xy$ C) $\dfrac{xy}{6}$ D) $\dfrac{600y}{x}$	

16. Try any two non-zero equal intercepts, such as $(1, 0)$ and $(0, 1)$. The slope is $(1 - 0)/(0 - 1) = -1$.	16. D
A) 0 B) even C) positive D) negative	

17. If $x \blacklozenge y = (x+y)^2 - xy$, then $4 \blacklozenge 2 = (4+2)^2 - (4)(2) = 36 - 8 = 28$.	17. B
A) 16 B) 28 C) 32 D) 36	

18. The area of such a square is π^2, the same as a circle of radius $\sqrt{\pi}$.	18. B
A) 1 B) $\sqrt{\pi}$ C) π D) π^2	

19. The product of 3 consecutive odd or even integers is divisible by 3.	19. D
A) $(x+1)(x+2)(x+4)$ B) $(x+2)(x+4)(x+5)$ C) $(x+3)(x+4)(x+6)$ D) $(x+4)(x+6)(x+8)$	

20. Patches the clown has 120 balloons, of which 5%, or 6, are blue. If he lets 90 of the balloons go but keep all the blue ones, then 6 of the 30 remaining ones are blue. As a percent, that's 20%.	20. B
A) 15% B) 20% C) 25% D) 30%	

21. If $x^{-1} = -\dfrac{1}{4}$, then $x^{-2} = (x^{-1})^2 = \left(-\dfrac{1}{4}\right)^2 = \dfrac{1}{16}$.	21. C
A) $-\dfrac{1}{2}$ B) $-\dfrac{1}{16}$ C) $\dfrac{1}{16}$ D) $\dfrac{1}{2}$	

22. If $(n-1)^2 = 81$, $n-1 = 9$ or -9, and $n-4 = 6$ or -12.	22. B
A) -14 B) -12 C) -10 D) -8	

Go on to the next page)))➡ **A**

23. An equation of the line that passes through the points (2,2) and (-4,4) is $y = -(1/3)x + 8/3$. Set y equal to 0 and solve for x to find x-intercept.

   A) (0,-8)   B) (8,0)   C) $(\frac{8}{3},0)$ D) $(0,-\frac{8}{3})$

24. Since QR is one-half of PQ, we have $4x - 6 = 2x$. Solving, $x = 3$. Thus, $PQ = 4x - 6 = 6$. Since PQ is half of PS, $PS = 12$.

   $\underset{\;}{P} \quad \underset{4x-6}{\;\;\;\;\;} \quad \underset{\;}{Q} \quad \underset{x}{\;} \quad \underset{\;}{R} \quad\quad \underset{\;}{S}$

   A) 2 cm   B) 3 cm   C) 6 cm   D) 12 cm

25. Let n = the number of students in Phillow's class. The sum of the scores of all the students in both classes is $82n + 86(60) = 82n + 5160$. The average of the two classes' scores is this sum divided by the total number of students (which is $n + 60$). Thus, $(82n + 5160)/(n + 60) = 85$. This is equivalent to $82n + 5160 = 85n + 5100$. Solving, $n = 20$.

   A) 20   B) 30   C) 40   D) 45

26. If x and y are primes and $\sqrt{3 \times 5} \times \sqrt{5 \times 7} \times \sqrt{xy}$ is a rational number, then $x + y$ equals $3 + 7 = 10$.

   A) 10   B) 13   C) 18   D) 21

27. $4^{31} \times 5^{61} = 2^{62} \times 5^{61} = 2 \times 2^{61} \times 5^{61} = 2 \times (2 \times 5)^{61} = 2 \times 10^{61}$.

   A) 30   B) 31   C) 60   D) 61

28. Look at consecutive powers of 7 until the ones digit is a 1. This first occurs when $x = 4$. It will happen again when $x = 8, 12, \ldots, 20, 24, \ldots$.

   A) 21   B) 22   C) 24   D) 25

29. Use the fact $3^n + 3^n + 3^n = 3^{n+1}$ repeatedly to get 3^{104}.

   A) 3^{104} B) 3^{105} C) 3^{110} D) 3^{910}

30. A hot dog eating champion set a new world record by eating x hot dogs in ten minutes. If there is only 1 solution to $2x^2 - bx + 9800 = 0$, $x^2 - (b/2)x + 4900$ is a perfect square, and $b/2$ must equal 140. Thus $b = 280$.

   A) -140   B) 70   C) 280   D) 490

The end of the contest **A**

Visit our Web site at http://www.mathleague.com

Information & Solutions

Spring, 2015

Contest Information

- **Solutions**   Turn the page for detailed contest solutions (written in the question boxes) and letter answers (written in the *Answer Column* to the right of each question).

- **Scores**   Please remember that *this is a contest, and not a test*—there is no "passing" or "failing" score. Few students score as high as 24 points (80% correct); students with half that, 12 points, *deserve commendation!*

- **Answers and Rating Scales**   Turn to page 151 for the letter answers to each question and the rating scale for this contest.

1. If $d = 8$, $r = 7$, $u = 6$, and $m = 5$, then
   $d - r + u - m = 8 - 7 + 6 - 5 = 2$.

   A) 2   B) 3   C) 4   D) 5

1.
A

2. If $x = -1$, $x^3 + 1 = -1 + 1 = 0$, $x^2 + 1 = 1 + 1 = 2$,
   and $x + 1 = -1 + 1 = 0$. The greatest value is 2.

   A) $x^3 + 1$ B) $x^2 + 1$ C) $x + 1$ D) 1

2.
B

3. $(x + 3x + 5x) + (2 + 4 + 6) = 9x + 12$.

   A) $3x + 21$ B) $7x + 8$ C) $8x + 10$ D) $9x + 12$

3.
D

4. $(t + 3)(t - 3)(t + 3)(t - 3) = (t^2 - 9)(t^2 - 9) = (t^2 - 9)^2$.

   A) $t^4 + 81$ B) $t^4 - 81$ C) $(t^2 - 9)^2$ D) $(t^2 + 9)^2$

4.
C

5. Substitute $x = -4$ in each choice and find the one that is equal to 0.

   A) $x^2 + 16$ B) $x^3 + 64$ C) $x^4 - 32$ D) $x^4 + 16$

5.
B

6. $(a + 4)(a - 3) - (a - 3)(a + 2) = (a - 3)[(a + 4) - (a + 2)] = (a - 3)(2)$.

   A) 2   B) 6   C) $2a + 2$ D) $2a + 6$

6.
A

7. $(50 - 1)(50 - 2)(50 - 3)(50 - 4) \ldots (50 - 49)(50 - 50) = 0$.

   A) 50!   B) 49!   C) 25^{25} D) 0

7.
D

8. $(x+y)^2 = x^2 + 2xy + y^2 = 100$. Since $x^2 + y^2 = 20$, $20 + 2xy = 100$; $xy = 40$.

   A) 2   B) 30   C) 40   D) 80

8.
C

9. $x\%$ of $\dfrac{100}{x} = \dfrac{x}{100} \times \dfrac{100}{x} = 1$.

   A) 1   B) x C) 100   D) $100x$

9.
A

10. There were $4c$ people crying and $7d$ people
    who weren't. If exactly half the people
    were crying, then $4c = 7d$. Therefore,
    $c:d = 7:4$.

    A) 4:7   B) 4:11   C) 7:4   D) 11:4

10.
C

11. $|2 - x^2| = |-x^2 + 2| = |-1(x^2 - 2)| = |x^2 - 2|$.

    A) $|2 + x^2|$ B) $|x^2 - 2|$ C) $2 + x^2$ D) $x^2 - 2$

11.
B

12. Since $x^4 \geq 0$, $x^4 + 1 > 0$.

    A) $x^2 - 1 = 0$ B) $x^3 + 1 = 0$ C) $x^4 - 1 = 0$ D) $x^4 + 1 = 0$

12.
D

Go on to the next page 〉〉〉▶ **A**

13. The perimeter of the rectangle is $2(\sqrt{8} + \sqrt{9}) = 2(2\sqrt{2}+3) = 6+4\sqrt{2}$. A) $6\sqrt{2}$ B) $6+4\sqrt{2}$ C) $\sqrt{17}$ D) $\sqrt{89}$	13. B
14. $[(x + 2)(x – 1)][(x + 1)(x – 2)] = (x^2 + x – 2) \times (x^2 – x – 2)$. A) x^2+x-2 B) x^2+x+2 C) x^2-x+2 D) x^2-x-2	14. D
15. The slope of $26x + 36y = 46$ is $-26/36 = -13/18$. Any parallel line must have the same slope. The slope of $39x + 54y = 23$ is $-39/54 = -13/18$. Since the slopes are equal, the lines are parallel.  A) $36x + 46y = 56$ B) $52x + 54y = 56$ C) $39x + 54y = 23$ D) $13x + 36y = 23$	15. C
16. The sum of 2 positive odd numbers is even. When a positive even number is divided by 2, the result must be a whole number. A) odd B) even C) prime D) whole	16. D
17. $\left(\dfrac{1}{x^2} + \dfrac{1}{x^3}\right) \div (x+1) = \left(\dfrac{x+1}{x^3}\right) \div (x+1) = \dfrac{1}{x^3}$. A) $\dfrac{1}{x^3}$ B) x^3 C) $\dfrac{1}{x^2}$ D) x^2	17. A
18. If $-2015 < x < 2015$, then $x = -2014, -2013, \ldots, 0, 1, 2, \ldots, 2014$. A) 2014 B) 4028 C) 4029 D) 4030	18. C
19. Yesterday I drove 40 km in 30 minutes. Today I will drive 50 km in 50 minutes. My average speed today in km/hr will be $50 \div (50/60) = 60$ km/hr. A) 40 B) 60 C) 70 D) 100	19. B
20. $5^{41} \times (2^2)^{21} = 5^{41} \times 2^{42} = 2 \times 5^{41} \times 2^{41} = 2 \times (5 \times 2)^{41} = 2 \times 10^{41}$. A) 11 B) 20 C) 21 D) 41	20. D
21. The circumference of the large circular end is $2\pi r = 1/(2r)$. Therefore, $r^2 = 1/(4\pi)$. Its area is $\pi r^2 = \pi \times 1/(4\pi) = 1/4$.  A) $\dfrac{1}{4\pi}$ B) $\dfrac{1}{2\pi}$ C) $\dfrac{1}{4}$ D) $\dfrac{1}{2}$	21. C
22. Since $|2x + 3| = 3x$, $3x \geq 0$ and $x \geq 0$. So $|2x + 3| = 2x + 3 = 3x$ and $x = 3$. A) 0 B) 1 C) 2 D) 4	22. B

Go on to the next page)))➡ **A**

23. If $y = 1 - x$, $x = 1 - y$. It follows that $x^2 = (1 - y)^2$ and $(1 - x)^2 = y^2$. A) $(1 - x)^2 = (1 - y)^2$ B) $(1 - x)^2 x^2 = (1 - y)^2 y^2$ C) $x^2 - (1 - x)^2 = y^2 - (1 - y)^2$ D) $(1 - x)^2 (1 + x)^2 = (1 - y)^2 (1 + y)$	23. B
24. Lee ate $0.01a + 0.02b + 0.03c$ grams of seed. Since this is 1.5% of all the feed, we have $(0.01a + 0.02b + 0.03c) \div (a + b + c) = 0.015$. Rewrite this as $a + 2b + 3c = 1.5a + 1.5b + 1.5c$. Hence $a = b + 3c$. A) $b + 3c$ B) $3b + c$ C) $2b + 3c$ D) $3b + 2c$	24. A
25. If $x^2 < 0.01$, $x^{-2} > 100$. This implies $x < -10$ for $x < 0$. A) less than -10 B) between -0.1 and 0 C) between 0 and 0.1 D) greater than 10	25. A
26. At 9:00 A.M., $r{:}b = 1{:}5$; thus, $b = 5r$. An hour later the number of red cars had increased by 2, the number of black cars had decreased by 5, and the ratio was $1{:}4$. Therefore, $(r + 2){:}(5r - 5) = 1{:}4$. Solving, we get $r = 13$, so $b = 5(13) = 65$; at 10 A.M., black cars $= 65 - 5 = 60$. A) 13 B) 15 C) 60 D) 65	26. C
27. $\dfrac{4x^3(x^2 - 1) - x^2 + 1}{(x+1)(x-1)} = \dfrac{4x^3(x^2 - 1) - (x^2 - 1)}{(x+1)(x-1)} = \dfrac{(4x^3 - 1)(x^2 - 1)}{x^2 - 1} = 4x^3 - 1$. A) $x^2 - 1$ B) $x^2 + 1$ C) $4x^2 + 1$ D) $4x^3 - 1$	27. D
28. Let r be the Camps' rate. The distance driven by 1:30 was $300 + 1.5r$; the distance by 3:30 was $300 + 3.5r$. Hence, $(300+1.5r)1.5 = 300+3.5r$. Thus $450 + 2.25r = 300 + 3.5r$, $1.25r = 150$ and their rate in km/hr is 120.  A) 150 B) 120 C) 100 D) 90	28. B
29. There are 10 positions the I's can be in and 4! places for the others. That's 10×24 in all. A) 240 B) 355 C) 600 D) 715	29. A
30. Let a, b, and c be the fraction of the house each can paint in 1 hour. Then $a + b = 1/12$, $a + c = 1/15$, and $b + c = 1/20$. Adding all 3 equations, we get $2a + 2b + 2c = 1/5$. Equivalently, $a + b + c = 1/10$. Thus, they paint 1/10 of the house in 1 hour and the entire house in 10 hours. A) 8.5 B) 9 C) 10 D) 10.5	30. C

The end of the contest **A**

Visit our Web site at http://www.mathleague.com

Information & Solutions

Spring, 2016

Contest Information

A

- **Solutions**   Turn the page for detailed contest solutions (written in the question boxes) and letter answers (written in the *Answer Column* to the right of each question).

- **Scores**   Please remember that *this is a contest, and not a test*—there is no "passing" or "failing" score. Few students score as high as 24 points (80% correct); students with half that, 12 points, *deserve commendation!*

- **Answers and Rating Scales**   Turn to page 152 for the letter answers to each question and the rating scale for this contest.

1. The sum of the cubes of the digits of 2016 is $2^3 + 1^3 + 6^3$. For each choice, the sum of the cubes of the digits is shown.
A) $1^3 + 6^3$ B) $1^3 + 6^3 + 2^3$ C) $2^3 + 1^3 + 6^3$ D) $6^3 + 2^3$

**1.
B**

2. If Tina registers and visits the gym n times, she will pay $50 for the one-time registration and $3n$ for her n visits. She will pay a total of $3n + 50$ dollars.

A) 53   B) $50n + 3$ C) $53n$ D) $3n + 50$

**2.

D**

3. $m^a \times t^h = 2^0 \times 1^6 = 1 \times 1 = 1$.

A) 0   B) 1   C) 2   D) 6

**3.
B**

4. Any even power of a number is ≥ 0. Adding 1 makes the sum > 0.
A) $x + 1$ B) $x^2 + 1$ C) $x^3 + 1$ D) x^{100}

**4.
B**

5. $(a-7)^2 - (a-3)(a-11) = (a^2 - 14a + 49) - (a^2 - 14a + 33) = 16$.
A) 16   B) $4a + 4$ C) $16a - 16$ D) $a^2 + 4a + 4$

**5.
A**

6. $\sqrt{1} + \sqrt{4} + \sqrt{9} + \sqrt{16} + \sqrt{25} = 1 + 2 + 3 + 4 + 5 = 15 = \sqrt{x}$. Square: $x = 225$.
A) 15   B) 20   C) 225   D) 400

**6.
C**

7. $x - 6$, $x + 6$, $x^2 - 49$, and $x^2 + 49$ equal 0 for 1, 1, 2, and 0 real numbers.
A) 2   B) 3   C) 4   D) 6

**7.
C**

8. We have $0.25y = 4x$. Multiplying both sides by 4, we get $y = 16x$.
A) $2x$ B) $4x$ C) $8x$ D) $16x$

**8.
D**

9. Suppose I bake c cakes and p pies. I use a total of $3c + 4p = 54$ cups of flour, and $5c + 2p = 48$ cups of sugar. Doubling the second equation, I get $3c + 4p = 54$ and $10c + 4p = 96$. Subtracting the first from the second, $7c = 42$. Therefore, $c = 6$.

A) 6   B) 7   C) 8   D) 9

**9.

A**

10. $x^2 - y^2 = (x + y)(x - y) = (30)(5) = 150$.

A) 35   B) -35   C) 150   D) -150

**10.
C**

11. $(x^6)^5 \times (x^{10})^2 = x^{30} \times x^{20} = x^{50}$.
A) x^{23} B) x^{50} C) x^{60} D) x^{600}

**11.
B**

12. If $x > 5$, then $|5 - x| + |x - 5| = (x - 5) + (x - 5) = 2(x - 5)$.
A) 0   B) 10   C) $2(5 - x)$ D) $2(x - 5)$

**12.
D**

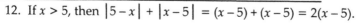

Go on to the next page)))→ **A**

13. The slopes of the four lines, in order, are -3, -1/3, 1, and -3/4. A) $y = -3x + 5$ B) $x = -3y + 5$ C) $-y - 3 = -x$ D) $3x + 4y = 5$	13. C
14. Jackie wants to switch to playing the triangle, so she studies triangles. If she finds a triangle with a base of $\sqrt{8}$ and a height of $\sqrt{18}$, the area of the triangle is $\sqrt{8} \times \sqrt{18}/2 = \sqrt{144}/2 = 12/2 = 6.$ A) 3 B) 6 C) 12 D) 144 	14. B
15. Lee asked Mo to pick any non-zero number x, square it, subtract x from the square, divide by x, and finally subtract x. The result was $\dfrac{x^2 - x}{x} - x = x - 1 - x = -1.$ A) -1 B) 1 C) x D) $-x$	15. A
16. $f(-1) = (-1 - 1)(-1 - 2) \ldots (-1 - 99) = (-2)(-3) \ldots (-100) = (-1)^{99}(100!).$ A) 100! B) -100! C) 101! D) -101!	16. B
17. $\left(\dfrac{1}{x+3} + \dfrac{1}{x+4}\right)(x^2 + 7x + 12) = \left(\dfrac{1}{x+3} + \dfrac{1}{x+4}\right)[(x+3)(x+4)] = (x+4) + (x+3) = 2x + 7.$ A) 7 B) $2x + 3$ C) $2x + 4$ D) $2x + 7$	17. D
18. If $x/5 = y/6 = z/7$, then when $x = 5$, $y = 6$ and $z = 7$. So $x : y : z = 5 : 6 : 7$. A) 7 : 6 : 5 B) 1/5 : 1/6 : 1/7 C) 5 : 6 : 7 D) 1/7 : 1/6 : 1/5	18. C
19. Let the numbers be a and b. Then, $1/a + 1/b = (a + b)/ab$. Since $a + b = 60$ and $ab = 15$, we have $60/15 = 4$. A) 4 B) 1/4 C) 6 D) 1/6	19. A
20. Suppose the one-way trip distance is 60 m. Andrew spends 2 s driving one way and 3 s driving the other way. He travels a total of 120 m. The average speed is $120/5 = 24$ m/s. A) 24 m/s B) 25 m/s C) 26 m/s D) 27 m/s 	20. A
21. The area of circle A is 4 times that of circle B. The area of circle B is 4 times that of circle C. The area of circle C is 4 times that of circle D. The area of circle A is $4 \times 4 \times 4 = 64$ times the area of circle D. A) 8 B) 16 C) 64 D) 256	21. C
22. Add exponents: $1 + 2 + 3 + \ldots + n = n(n+1)/2 = 2016$. Try answers. A) 62 B) 63 C) 64 D) 65	22. B

Go on to the next page))⟩ **A**

23. Jean's total would be $1 after Day 1, $3 after Day 2, $7 after Day 3, etc. The pattern is that after the nth day, she has a total of $\$2^n - \$1$. Continuing every day for exactly 4 weeks means that $n = 28$. Jean would have a total of $\$2^{28} - \$1$ after 28 days.

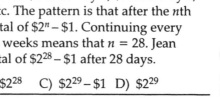

A) $\$2^{28} - \$1$ B) $\$2^{28}$ C) $\$2^{29} - \$1$ D) $\$2^{29}$

23.

A

24. $a^2 - a = b^2 - b$; $a^2 - b^2 = a - b$. Divide $(a - b)$: $a + b = 1$.

A) b B) $-b$ C) $b - 1$ D) $1 - b$

24.

D

25. $23 < x^2 < 293$; $5 \le |x| \le 17$. 13 positive, 13 negative.

A) 12   B) 13   C) 24   D) 26

25.

D

26. Generalize:1 prime, 2 divisors; 2 primes, 2^2 divisors; 3 primes, 2^3 divisors.

A) 2017   B) 2018   C) 2^{2016} D) 2^{2017}

26.

C

27. Let N be the numerator and D be the denominator of the original fraction. $(N - 1)/D = 3/5$ and $N/(D + 22) = 1/2$. Cross-multiplying, $5(N - 1) = 3D$ and $2N = D + 22$. Isolating D in each, $3D = 5N - 5$ and $D = 2N - 22$. Triple the second equation and subtract to get $N = 61$, and then $D = 100$. The new fraction is $(N + 5)/(D + 5) = 66/105 = 22/35$.

A) 22/35   B) 31/50   C) 36/73   D) 56/79

27.

A

28. The probability that the first ball chosen is red is 1/2, so the probability that the second ball chosen is red is $9/38 \div 1/2 = 9/19$. If there are $2n$ balls in the box initially, the probability that the second ball chosen is red is $(n-1)/(2n-1)$. Thus, $9/19 = (n-1)/(2n-1)$ and $n = 10$.

A) 10   B) 20   C) 22   D) 24

28.

A

29. Let S be the number of stalks of broccoli, B be the number of bananas, and R be the number of oranges. We have $5S + 4B + 8R = 5.60$ and $7S + 3B + 10R = 7$. To get the value of $3S + 5B + 6R$, double the 1st equation and subtract the 2nd equation.

A) $1.40   B) $2.80   C) $4.20   D) $5.60

29.

C

30. "Glue" Al and Barb as one person and Cy and Di as another. There are $5! = 120$ ways for 5 people to stand in a line. "Glued" people can each stand in 2 ways. The answer is $120 \times 2 \times 2 = 480$.

A) 240   B) 480   C) 1260   D) 5040

30.

B

The end of the contest **A**

Answer Keys & Difficulty Ratings

2011-2012 through 2015-2016

ANSWERS, 2011-12 7th Grade Contest

1. B	8. A	15. A	22. C	29. C
2. A	9. D	16. B	23. A	30. B
3. B	10. A	17. D	24. A	31. C
4. C	11. B	18. D	25. D	32. D
5. D	12. B	19. C	26. A	33. B
6. C	13. D	20. A	27. A	34. A
7. A	14. C	21. B	28. D	35. B

RATE YOURSELF!!!
for the 2011-12 7th GRADE CONTEST

Score	Rating
33-35	Another Einstein
30-32	Mathematical Wizard
27-29	School Champion
24-26	Grade Level Champion
21-23	Best In The Class
18-20	Excellent Student
16-17	Good Student
13-15	Average Student
0-12	Better Luck Next Time

ANSWERS, 2012-13 7th Grade Contest

1. D	8. A	15. A	22. D	29. B
2. B	9. D	16. D	23. C	30. C
3. B	10. D	17. D	24. C	31. C
4. A	11. A	18. A	25. C	32. D
5. A	12. B	19. B	26. C	33. C
6. C	13. C	20. B	27. A	34. C
7. C	14. C	21. C	28. C	35. A

RATE YOURSELF!!!
for the 2012-13 7th GRADE CONTEST

Score		Rating
34-35		Another Einstein
31-33		Mathematical Wizard
28-30		School Champion
25-27		Grade Level Champion
22-24		Best In The Class
19-21		Excellent Student
17-18		Good Student
14-16		Average Student
0-13		Better Luck Next Time

ANSWERS, 2013-14 7th Grade Contest

1. A	8. A	15. C	22. A	29. A
2. D	9. A	16. D	23. C	30. B
3. C	10. A	17. A	24. B	31. A
4. B	11. B	18. B	25. C	32. D
5. B	12. D	19. B	26. D	33. A
6. C	13. B	20. A	27. D	34. C
7. D	14. D	21. C	28. A	35. B

RATE YOURSELF!!!
for the 2013-14 7th GRADE CONTEST

Score	Rating
34-35	Another Einstein
32-33	Mathematical Wizard
30-31	School Champion
27-29	Grade Level Champion
25-26	Best In The Class
22-24	Excellent Student
19-21	Good Student
16-18	Average Student
0-15	Better Luck Next Time

ANSWERS, 2014-15 7th Grade Contest

1. C	8. B	15. A	22. B	29. B
2. B	9. A	16. C	23. A	30. B
3. D	10. D	17. D	24. C	31. C
4. A	11. D	18. A	25. C	32. D
5. B	12. C	19. D	26. B	33. C
6. C	13. A	20. B	27. B	34. C
7. A	14. B	21. D	28. A	35. D

RATE YOURSELF!!!
for the 2014-15 7th GRADE CONTEST

Score	Rating
33-35	Another Einstein
30-32	Mathematical Wizard
27-29	School Champion
24-26	Grade Level Champion
21-23	Best In The Class
18-20	Excellent Student
15-17	Good Student
12-14	Average Student
0-11	Better Luck Next Time

ANSWERS, 2015-16 7th Grade Contest

1. C	8. B	15. A	22. D	29. C
2. D	9. D	16. C	23. A	30. A
3. D	10. A	17. C	24. C	31. A
4. C	11. A	18. A	25. B	32. D
5. A	12. D	19. C	26. D	33. B
6. B	13. D	20. B	27. B	34. C
7. A	14. B	21. D	28. A	35. D

RATE YOURSELF!!!
for the 2015-16 7th GRADE CONTEST

Score	Rating
34-35	Another Einstein
32-33	Mathematical Wizard
29-31	School Champion
26-28	Grade Level Champion
23-25	Best In The Class
21-22	Excellent Student
18-20	Good Student
15-17	Average Student
0-14	Better Luck Next Time

ANSWERS, 2011-12 8th Grade Contest

1. B	8. C	15. A	22. D	29. B
2. B	9. C	16. D	23. D	30. C
3. B	10. B	17. B	24. C	31. B
4. C	11. C	18. A	25. A	32. C
5. D	12. A	19. A	26. D	33. D
6. A	13. B	20. B	27. D	34. A
7. D	14. C	21. D	28. D	35. A

RATE YOURSELF!!!
for the 2011-12 8th GRADE CONTEST

Score	Rating
34-35	Another Einstein
32-33	Mathematical Wizard
30-31	School Champion
28-29	Grade Level Champion
25-27	Best In The Class
22-24	Excellent Student
19-21	Good Student
16-18	Average Student
0-15	Better Luck Next Time

ANSWERS, 2012-13 8th Grade Contest

1. C	8. C	15. A	22. C	29. D
2. D	9. C	16. B	23. B	30. C
3. D	10. D	17. C	24. D	31. A
4. B	11. B	18. A	25. D	32. A
5. C	12. C	19. D	26. A	33. B
6. A	13. B	20. B	27. B	34. C
7. D	14. C	21. B	28. A	35. C

RATE YOURSELF!!!
for the 2012-13 8th GRADE CONTEST

Score	Rating
34-35	Another Einstein
32-33	Mathematical Wizard
29-31	School Champion
26-28	Grade Level Champion
23-25	Best In The Class
20-22	Excellent Student
17-19	Good Student
15-16	Average Student
0-14	Better Luck Next Time

ANSWERS, 2013-14 8th Grade Contest

1. B	8. D	15. B	22. D	29. A
2. B	9. D	16. A	23. A	30. D
3. C	10. D	17. A	24. D	31. B
4. A	11. A	18. B	25. D	32. C
5. D	12. D	19. C	26. C	33. C
6. A	13. B	20. D	27. D	34. A
7. B	14. B	21. B	28. B	35. B

RATE YOURSELF!!!
for the 2013-14 8th GRADE CONTEST

Score	Rating
34-35	Another Einstein
32-33	Mathematical Wizard
30-31	School Champion
27-29	Grade Level Champion
25-26	Best In The Class
22-24	Excellent Student
19-21	Good Student
16-18	Average Student
0-15	Better Luck Next Time

ANSWERS, 2014-15 8th Grade Contest

1. D	8. D	15. B	22. B	29. C
2. C	9. C	16. C	23. A	30. A
3. A	10. B	17. A	24. C	31. D
4. B	11. A	18. D	25. D	32. B
5. A	12. B	19. B	26. D	33. B
6. D	13. A	20. D	27. A	34. A
7. C	14. C	21. C	28. C	35. C

RATE YOURSELF!!!
for the 2014-15 8th GRADE CONTEST

Score	Rating
33-35	Another Einstein
30-32	Mathematical Wizard
28-29	School Champion
25-27	Grade Level Champion
22-24	Best In The Class
19-21	Excellent Student
17-18	Good Student
14-16	Average Student
0-13	Better Luck Next Time

ANSWERS, 2015-16 8th Grade Contest

1. B	8. B	15. B	22. D	29. B
2. C	9. B	16. D	23. B	30. A
③ B	10. D	17. C	24. D	31. B
4. A	11. C	18. A	25. C	32. D
5. C	12. A	19. C	26. A	33. A
6. D	13. C	20. A	27. B	34. B
7. A	⑭ A	21. B	28. A	35. C

RATE YOURSELF!!!
for the 2015-16 8th GRADE CONTEST

Score	Rating
33-35	Another Einstein
30-32	Mathematical Wizard
27-29	School Champion
24-26	Grade Level Champion
21-23	Best In The Class
19-20	Excellent Student
16-18	Good Student
13-15	Average Student
0-12	Better Luck Next Time

ANSWERS, 2011-12 Algebra Course 1 Contest

1. A	7. C	13. C	19. D	25. B
2. B	8. D	14. D	20. B	26. C
3. D	9. B	15. A	21. C	27. C
4. B	10. A	16. A	22. B	28. A
5. C	11. D	17. B	23. D	29. B
6. C	12. C	18. C	24. C	30. A

RATE YOURSELF!!!
for the 2011-12 ALGEBRA COURSE 1 CONTEST

Score	Rating
28-30	Another Einstein
24-27	Mathematical Wizard
21-23	School Champion
19-20	Grade Level Champion
17-18	Best In The Class
14-16	Excellent Student
12-13	Good Student
9-11	Average Student
0-8	Better Luck Next Time

ANSWERS, 2012-13 Algebra Course 1 Contest

1. B	7. B	13. C	19. B	25. A
2. C	8. D	14. A	20. B	26. A
3. C	9. C	15. D	21. C	27. D
4. A	10. B	16. D	22. D	28. D
5. A	11. D	17. B	23. A	29. C
6. D	12. B	18. D	24. B	30. C

RATE YOURSELF!!!
for the 2012-13 ALGEBRA COURSE 1 CONTEST

Score	Rating
29-30	Another Einstein
27-28	Mathematical Wizard
24-26	School Champion
21-23	Grade Level Champion
19-20	Best In The Class
16-18	Excellent Student
13-15	Good Student
10-12	Average Student
0-9	Better Luck Next Time

ANSWERS, 2013-14 Algebra Course 1 Contest

1. D	7. C	13. D	19. D	25. A
2. A	8. D	14. A	20. B	26. A
3. C	9. A	15. C	21. C	27. D
4. B	10. A	16. D	22. B	28. C
5. A	11. B	17. B	23. B	29. A
6. B	12. C	18. B	24. D	30. C

RATE YOURSELF!!!
for the 2013-14 ALGEBRA COURSE 1 CONTEST

Score		Rating
28-30		Another Einstein
25-27		Mathematical Wizard
22-24		School Champion
19-21		Grade Level Champion
16-18		Best In The Class
14-15		Excellent Student
12-13		Good Student
9-11		Average Student
0-8		Better Luck Next Time

ANSWERS, 2014-15 Algebra Course 1 Contest

1. A	7. D	13. B	19. B	25. A
2. B	8. C	14. D	20. D	26. C
3. D	9. A	15. C	21. C	27. D
4. C	10. C	16. D	22. B	28. B G
5. B	11. B	17. A	23. B	29. A
6. A	12. D	18. C	24. A	30. C

RATE YOURSELF!!!
for the 2014-15 ALGEBRA COURSE 1 CONTEST

Score		Rating
28-30		Another Einstein
25-27		Mathematical Wizard
22-24		School Champion
19-21		Grade Level Champion
16-18		Best In The Class
14-15		Excellent Student
11-13		Good Student
10-12		Average Student
0-9		Better Luck Next Time

ANSWERS, 2015-16 Algebra Course 1 Contest

1. B	7. C	13. C	19. A	25. D
2. D	8. D	14. B	20. A	26. C
3. B	9. A	15. A	21. C	27. A
4. B	10. C	16. B	22. B	28. A
5. A	11. B	17. D	23. A	29. C
6. C	12. D	18. C	24. D	30. B

RATE YOURSELF!!!
for the 2015-16 ALGEBRA COURSE 1 CONTEST

Score	Rating
29-30	Another Einstein
26-28	Mathematical Wizard
23-25	School Champion
20-22	Grade Level Champion
17-19	Best In The Class
15-16	Excellent Student
12-14	Good Student
9-11	Average Student
0-8	Better Luck Next Time

Math League Contest Books
4th Grade Through High School Levels

Written by Steven Conrad & Daniel Flegler, recipients of Ronald Reagan's 1985 Presidential Awards for Excellence in Mathematics Teaching

Order books at www.mathleague.com (or use the form below)

Name: _____

Address: _____

City: _____ State: _____ Zip: _____

Available Titles	# of Copies	Cost
Math Contests—Grades 4, 5, 6	($12.95 each)	
Volume 1: 1979-80 through 1985-86	_____	_____
Volume 2: 1986-87 through 1990-91	_____	_____
Volume 3: 1991-92 through 1995-96	_____	_____
Volume 4: 1996-97 through 2000-01	_____	_____
Volume 5: 2001-02 through 2005-06	_____	_____
Volume 6: 2006-07 through 2010-11	_____	_____
Volume 7: 2011-12 through 2015-16	_____	_____
Math Contests—Grades 7 & 8 ‡ ‡(Vols. 3,4,5,6,7 include Alg. Course 1)		
Volume 1: 1977-78 through 1981-82	_____	_____
Volume 2: 1982-83 through 1990-91	_____	_____
Volume 3: 1991-92 through 1995-96	_____	_____
Volume 4: 1996-97 through 2000-01	_____	_____
Volume 5: 2001-02 through 2005-06	_____	_____
Volume 6: 2006-07 through 2010-11	_____	_____
Volume 7: 2011-12 through 2015-16	_____	_____
Math Contests—High School		
Volume 1: 1977-78 through 1981-82	_____	_____
Volume 2: 1982-83 through 1990-91	_____	_____
Volume 3: 1991-92 through 1995-96	_____	_____
Volume 4: 1996-97 through 2000-01	_____	_____
Volume 5: 2001-02 through 2005-06	_____	_____
Volume 6: 2006-07 through 2010-11	_____	_____
Volume 7: 2011-12 through 2015-16	_____	_____
Shipping and Handling	$3 ($5 Canadian)	

Please allow 2-4 weeks for delivery   Total: $_____

☐ Check or Purchase Order Enclosed; **or**

☐ Visa / MC / Amex # _____ Expires _____

☐ Security Code _____ Signature _____

Mail your order with payment to:
Math League Press. PO Box 17, Tenafly, New Jersey USA 07670-0017
or order on the Web at www.mathleague.com

Phone: (201) 568-6328 • Fax: (201) 816-0125